THE KNIGHTS HOSPITALLER IN

GREAT BRITAIN IN 1540

THE KNIGHTS HOSPITALLER IN GREAT BRITAIN IN 1540

A Survey of the Houses and Churches etc of St John of Jerusalem including those earlier belonging to the Knights Templar

by

Michael Hodges

With photographs by the author

MOUNT ORLEANS PRESS

IN PIAM MEMORIAM PROFESSOR JONATHAN RILEY-SMITH, SOMETIME DIXIE PROFESSOR OF ECCLESIASTICAL HISTORY AT THE UNIVERSITY OF CAMBRIDGE, KNIGHT GRAND CROSS OF GRACE AND DEVOTION OF THE SOVEREIGN MILITARY ORDER OF MALTA, AND DR MAURICE KEEN, SOMETIME MEDIEVAL HISTORY FELLOW AT BALLIOL ❧ COLLEGE, OXFORD ☙

Frontispiece: Pleurant of a Knight of Rhodes from the tomb of Sir Ralph Fitzherbert (obit 1483) depicting his son Richard in the Church of St Mary and St Barlock, Norbury, Derbyshire.

First published in 2018 by The Grand Priory of England, Order of Malta
This edition published 2019 by Mount Orleans Press,
23 High Street, Cricklade, SN6 6AP
https://anthonyeyre.com

© 2018 Michael Hodges

All rights reserved. No part of this publication may be reproduced,
stored in a retrieval system, or transmitted in any form or by any means,
electronic, mechanical, photocopying or otherwise, without
the prior permission of the copyright holder.

CIP data for this title are available from the British Library

Typography and book production by Anthony Eyre

ISBN 978-1-91294-513-9

Printed in Italy

CONTENTS

FOREWORD 7

PREFACE 9

INTRODUCTION 11

GAZETTEER:
ENGLAND, SCOTLAND
AND WALES 23

IRELAND 148

INDEX OF PLACES 149

FOREWORD

Fra' Ian Scott, 57th Grand Prior of England

THE ORIGINS OF THE ORDER of St John of Jerusalem, of Rhodes and of Malta, commonly known as the Order of Malta, go back to 1048 when a group of merchants from Amalfi set up a hospital in Jerusalem. This subsequently became an independent entity under Blessed Gerard, regarded as the founder of the Order. The Order served a hospital for travellers to the Holy Land, and later it came to defend pilgrims from attack. The aims of the Order remain the same to this day: 'Tuitio Fidei et Obsequium Pauperum', the protection of the Catholic faith and help for the poor and the oppressed.

Under his successor, Raymond de Puy, the Order grew and across Europe 'commanderies', each under the authority of a celibate knight, were established to support the works of the Order. The commandery provided a living for the knight and his dependents. In addition, a percentage of the profits was sent to the Order's headquarters to maintain the military and hospitaller activities in the Mediterranean. The commanderies were mostly modest in size, consisting of a chapel, living accommodation and farm buildings. In England they covered most counties, and quickly became a prominent feature of the religious life of the countryside. They had a duty of hospitality to strangers, and also welcomed pilgrims on their way to the great medieval centres in Great Britain and overseas, and dispensed charity to the poor and the needy.

In 1312, after the suppression of the Knights Templar, the Order of St John was granted the majority of their properties and became the greatest landowner in the Kingdom after the monarch. The Grand Prior of England, who claimed authority over the whole of the British Isles, sat as a baron in the House of Lords, and was accorded the senior rank.

Following the Protestant Reformation, the Order became a natural target for Henry VIII, and the Order was suppressed in this country in 1546 and all its property confiscated. Briefly revived under Mary Tudor and James II, the Order was finally re-established in 1876 and the Grand Priory revived in 1993 with Fra' Matthew Festing as Grand Prior.

Many of the commanderies now lie in ruins, some few are still working farms, whilst others have become parish churches or have been incorporated into private houses. This book will be a wonderful resource for people to deepen their understanding of the Order in England. This is the first definitive record of the many buildings that formed such an integral part of the medieval life of our country. I congratulate the author on his erudition and stamina in tracking down these dwellings, and upon the wonderful photographic record he offers us, and am truly delighted to recommend it to all who are interested in medieval history and the history of the Order of Malta in this country.

FRA' IAN SCOTT   *Feast of St Edmund*
                                              the Martyr, 2017

Opposite: Pleurant of a Knight of Rhodes from the tomb of Sir Thomas Babington (obit 1518) depicting his son John in the Church of All Saints, Ashover, Derbyshire.

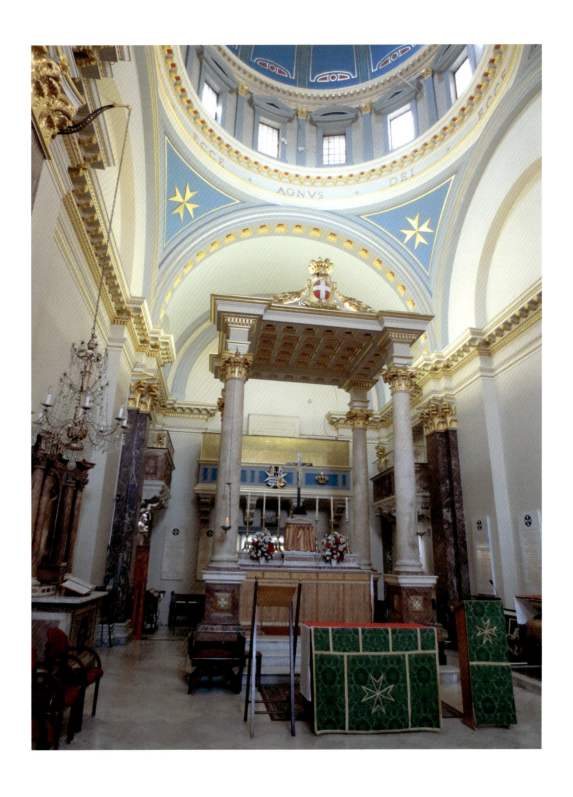

The Church of St John of Jerusalem, Hospital of St John and Elizabeth, St John's Wood.

PREFACE

THE GRAND PRIOR OF ENGLAND, Fra' Ian Scott, originally asked me if I would consider undertaking this task in the spring of 2016. I agreed and spent a fairly arduous summer working mainly through the Victoria County Histories and the Pevsner *Architectural Guides*. At the same time I started photographing the remnants of the various commanderies belonging to, and those churches appropriated to, the Knights Hospitaller in order to record their architectural legacy as it might have been in 1540.

I must first and foremost thank Pamela Willis of the Museum and Library of the Order of St John in Clerkenwell who has been extremely generous in providing me with copies of her very detailed notes on the possessions of the Knights Hospitaller in the English counties. Without her this book (which I suspect she regards as sadly lightweight) would not have been possible.

I am very grateful to those who have accompanied me on various excursions. These include, first and foremost, my wife Veronica, but I must also mention, in alphabetical order, Mr Nicholas and Mrs Carol Bennett, Mr Alan Black, H.E. Fra' Matthew Festing, Sir Josslyn and Lady (Jane) Gore-Booth, Mr Patrick Mackie, Mrs Gail Mooney, Dr John Martin Robinson, Fra' Ian Scott and Mr Peter Sefton-Williams.

I am also very grateful to those who have provided accommodation and hospitality on our travels. These include, again in alphabetical order, Mr Nicholas and Mrs Carol Bennett, Mr and Mrs James Cockburn, Lord and Lady (Quentin and Chantal) Davies of Stamford, Her Serene Highness Princess Charles (Sarah) de Rohan (who arranged access to Dinmore in Herefordshire), H.E. Fra' Matthew Festing, Sir Josslyn and Lady Gore-Booth, Lady Celestria Hales, Mr Nicky and Mrs Rita Hodges, Mr Charles and Mrs Veronica Lillis (who arranged access to Halston in Shropshire), Mr Patrick Mackie, Mr Brian and Mrs Gail Mooney, Mr Jonathan and the Hon Mrs Selina Peto, Dr John Martin Robinson, Mr David and Mrs Caroline Wakefield and Mr Fred and Mrs Debbie West.

I am very grateful to the following, again in alphabetical order, who have provided me with information and/or photographs: Mr Kenneth Cameron, Mr Herbert Coutts, Mr Anthony Delarue, Mr Liam Devlin, Mr Angus Hay, Mr Chris Knock and Mr Desmond Seward.

I am very grateful to Mr Alan Black for proof reading the text.

Bibliographically, I am deeply indebted to the various *Victoria County Histories*, Pevsner *Architectural Guides*, the *Shell County Guides* and individual church guides too numerous to list. In addition I have consulted:

The Order of the Hospital of St John of Jerusalem by W.K.R.Bedford and Lieutenant Richard Holbeche (F.E.Robinson and Co 1902)

The Knights Hospitaller of the English Langue by Gregory O'Malley (Oxford University Press 2005)

The Priors of the Knights Hospitaller in Late Medieval England by Simon Phillips (Boydell 2009)

Hospitallers: History of the Order of St John by Jonathan Riley-Smith (Bloomsbury 1999)

The Monks of War: The Military Religious Orders by Desmond Seward (Eyre Methuen 1972)

The Knights of Malta by Henry Sire (Yale University Press 1996)

The Knights Hospitaller in England Being the Report of Prior Philip de Thame to the Grand Master Elyan de Villanova AD *1338* (Camden Society 1857)

*Krak des Chevaliers, Syria
(Omar Sanadiki/Reuters)*

INTRODUCTION

THE KNIGHTS HOSPITALLER IN JERUSALEM, RHODES AND MALTA

The origins of the Knights Hospitaller go back to c1070 when a Hospital of St John the Almoner was set up in Jerusalem (under Moslem control since 681) by merchants from Amalfi to cater for the needs of poor male pilgrims who were sick. It was founded as a daughter house of the Cassinese Benedictine Abbey of St Mary of the Latins. In 1099 Jerusalem was seized from its Moslem rulers by a crusader army under Count Raymond IV of Toulouse and Godfrey de Bouillon. The Latin Kingdom of Jerusalem was set up as well as the counties of Edessa and Tripoli and the Principality of Antioch.

In c1100 a certain Fra' Gerard from Amalfi, about whom little is known, was elected Master of the Hospital. He abandoned the Benedictine for the Augustine rule and adopted St John the Baptist as patron. In 1113 the freedom of the Hospital was confirmed by Pope Pascal II in the Bull *Pie Postulatio Voluntatis*.

In c1120 the Templars were set up under Hugues de Payens as a military order. They fought to defend Christians and the Holy Places. One of the seven promises the Templars made on profession was to 'help conquer... the Holy Land and to keep and save whatever Christians hold'. The four promises made by a Hospitaller on profession contained no reference to fighting or the defence of Christendom.

Fra' Gerard died c1120 and was succeeded by Raymond de Puy. The Order's nursing work had already made it rich and popular, with more than 1000 pilgrims a year being accommodated in Jerusalem. It received grants of land locally but also in Western Europe. Anastasius IV gave the Hospitallers their own priests and the English Pope Adrian IV their own churches. In 1126 a Constable of the Order is mentioned which implies some kind of military organisation. In 1136 King Fulk of Jerusalem gave them their first castle, Gibelin. By 1187 they controlled more than twenty strongholds in Outremer. The greatest of these, Krak des Chevaliers, in modern Syria, was given to them by Count Raymond II of Tripoli in 1142. In 1178 a bull of Alexander III stated they could only bear arms when the standard of the cross was displayed. Commanderies (or preceptories; I use the former term for convenience and consistency), small units of knights administering adjoining groups of properties, were set up in Europe and grouped into priories. They were exempt from episcopal control. Donations of lands to the Hospitallers began in Provence and Spain in the first third of the 12th century. In the middle third of the 12th century donations spread to France and England. After the Second Crusade (1147-8) donations became more general throughout Christendom.

In 1187 the Kurdish Saladin, who ruled both Cairo and Damascus, crossed the River Jordan with an army of 60,000 and defeated Guy de Lusignan, the King of Jerusalem, (assisted by both Hospitaller and Templar Knights) at the Battle of Hattin. Jerusalem and Acre fell, and the Hospitallers moved their headquarters to Tyre.

In 1191 Richard Coeur de Lion and King Philip Augustus of France arrived in the Holy Land on the Third Crusade. Acre was recaptured and Saladin defeated at the Battle of Ascalon. Thereafter a truce was signed which however left Jerusalem in Moslem hands, although from the 1220s to 1244 the Christians re-established control. In 1206 the Hospitallers established their headquarters in Acre. Robert L'Anglais was Grand Commander from 1195 to 1201, the first Englishman of note in the Order.

By the 13th century the militarisation of the Hospitallers was complete. It was ordained that commanderies had to send one third of their revenues to Outremer for the military use of the Order. By 1268 the so-called Langues had emerged. These were quasi collegiate corporations of brothers at the Order's headquarters, representing European groups of commanderies and priories. There came to be seven Langues: Provence, Auvergne, France, Italy, Spain, England and Germany. In 1330 various roles were allocated to the Langues; that of England provided the Turcopolier who originally in the Holy Land had commanded the light cavalry recruited from the local population. He subsequently became responsible for the coastguard in Rhodes, then Malta. While in theory supposed to be based at the Convent in Rhodes, succeeding Turcopoliers tended to spend an increasing amount of time in England.

The Kingdom of Jerusalem increasingly tottered during the course of the last half of the 13th century. In 1271 Krak des Chevaliers fell. In 1291 Acre yielded to a vast Mameluke army; this marked the effective end of the Latin Kingdom of Jerusalem.

The headquarters of the Order moved initially to Limassol in Cyprus. At this stage there were only 65 knights in the island, five of them English. In 1306 the Knights Hospitaller seized Rhodes from the Byzantine Emperor. Three years later their headquarters was moved there. The Order now became a maritime power for the first time.

In 1307 Philippe le Bel of France with his Chancellor Guillaume de Nogaret moved against the Templars, primarily for financial reasons. The Grand Master, Jacques de Molay, was arrested and accused of denial of Christ, idol worship, spitting on the cross and homosexuality. The French Pope, Clement V, in Avignon ordered the arrest of all Templars. 120, including the Grand Master, were burnt to death in France, and the Order was dissolved. Their lands were in the main given to the Hospitallers. It took many years for the latter to get hold of them, but it represented a vast accretion of wealth.

Rhodes became increasingly vulnerable during the course of the 15th century. The first great siege took place in 1446. There was a further unsuccessful assault in 1479 but eventually a successful one by Suleiman the Magnificent in 1522. In 1531 the Order accepted the offer of Malta from King Charles V. By the time of the Great Siege of Malta in 1565 the Grand Priory of England had ceased to exist in its homeland. The Langue was eventually dissolved in 1631.

THE KNIGHTS HOSPITALLER IN ENGLAND

In England in the early 12th century the Knights Templar, presumably because of their glamorous fighting role, were initially more successful in attracting donations of land after their arrival in England in 1128, and this position was maintained until the accession of Henry II in 1154. The English Hospitaller Priory was initially controlled from St Gilles in France. However there were some donations to the Hospitallers before 1154 and Robert, Earl of Derby (died 1139) and Gilbert, Earl of Hertford (died 1152) are for instance listed as early benefactors. The Commandery of Godsfield in Hampshire was presented by Henry of Blois, brother of King Stephen and Bishop of Winchester from 1129 to 1171. The Clares (variously Earls of Hertford, Pembroke and Striguil (Essex)) were particularly generous and gave the very wealthy Commandery of Slebech in Pembrokeshire as well as those at Carbrooke (Norfolk), Melchbourne (Bedfordshire) and Standon (Hertfordshire). Some 2000 separate properties from 1140 onwards were given to the Hospitallers in England and Wales.

The reason why lands were given to the two orders is summed up by this statement of 1139 'William de Braose to all his men of the castelry of Brembre (Bramber in Sussex), as well clerks as laymen, and all the sons of Holy Mother Church. Know that I have confirmed the gift that my mother Anor (Eleanor) gave for the soul of my father Philip and for the souls of our ancestors and for the redemption of our sinning selves to the Knights of Solomon's Temple (ie The Templars)…' John de Basing, the son of the initial benefactor to the Hospitallers at Sutton-at-Hone (Kent) also stated 'I, John de Basyngges, the son of Robert de Bassynes (sic)… moved with divine love and for the salvation of my soul, and the souls of my antecessors and successors, give…to God, the blessed Mary, and S.John the Baptist, and the blessed poor of the holy house of the Hospital of Jerusalem and the brethren of the house at Sutton att Hone sojourning there, and serving God, all of my land… to the foresaid brethren and their successors for free, pure and perpetual alms…' Donations tended to be made by knights who had been on crusade or by those salving their conscience for not going on crusade.

The first charter of the Knights Hospitaller in England was granted in 1155. It was the visit of the Master, Roger de Moulins, along with Heraclius, the Patriarch of Jerusalem, to seek help for the Holy Land in 1185 that brought the Order to the fore. St John's Priory, Clerkenwell was consecrated by them and the English Priory became free from St Gilles. Richard I was a supporter of the Hospitallers because of their assistance to him during the Third Crusade. He had worked closely with Garnier de Nablous who from 1189/90 was Grand Commander of France and Prior of England, and subsequently became Master of the Order. Richard I granted the Priory a beneficial charter in 1194; he also put hospitals in Hereford and Worcester under its care.

The Hospitallers thus steadily acquired lands in England between the 1140s and the signing of the Statute of Mortmain in 1279 which made grants to religious houses subject to royal licence. The Hospitallers possessed land in all the counties of England but their holdings were concentrated, to at least half in terms of income, in Cambridgeshire, Essex, Kent, Lincolnshire, Yorkshire and London.

The Priory maintained good relations with John and Henry III, undertaking various diplomatic missions for the latter. Edward I made the Prior Joseph de Chauncy his Treasurer from 1273-80 although in 1295 financial problems made the former attempt to seize the property of the Priory; he backed down under pressure from the Papacy. By 1299 the Hospitallers had 28 commanderies in England.

In 1236-9 knights were given precedence over priests serving in commanderies. In 1262 it was ordained that knights must be of noble birth and arms.

In 1268 England was mentioned in a magistral letter as being one of the Order's richest sources of revenue. It in fact provided c12.5% of European revenues. The senior officer was the Prior of England, known as 'My Lord of St John's', based in Clerkenwell. He was an important figure in English life, given precedence in the House of Lords before all lay barons (but of course after the greater nobles). He sat on the King's Council and was from time to time given military and ministerial roles.

The Knights Templar and the Knights Hospitaller held a unique position in the realm that they were not liable to pay any of the normal taxes of the land to the King nor did they pay ecclesiastical taxes. For instance the military orders were exempt in 1275 when Pope Gregory X levied a tax of 10% of the value of all clerical and lay property. Their churches also continuing functioning when the country as a whole was put under an interdict by the Pope.

The commanderies and estates of the Templars were valued at c£7,000 in 1308; Yorkshire (nine commanderies) at £1,400 and Lincolnshire (five commanderies) at £900 were the most valuable counties.

With the dissolution of the Templars in 1312 the papal bull *Vox in Excelso* issued by Pope Clement V granted the lands of the Templars to the Hospitallers. This countermanded in England the intentions of Edward II who in 1309 had written to the Treasurer and the Barons of the Exchequer 'We wish to have a true value of all lands and buildings of the Templars… we will take into our own hands.' The number of commanderies in England went up from thirty to forty five. It took until 1329 for all the Templar properties to be handed over. The Prior from 1318 to 1328 was Thomas l'Archer, who found the situation overwhelming, weighed down as he was by 'age and corpulence'; one sympathises. The Knights Hospitaller were anyway by 1338 the greatest individual ecclesiastical landlord in England in the later Middle Ages, followed probably by Glastonbury Abbey.

Many churches were appropriated to the Hospitallers who usually retained the great tithes (corn, hay and wood), the small tithes (livestock, butter cheese, fruit, vegetables, honey, wax, flax, wool, hemp, rushes, game and fish), altar dues, funeral, offerings, oblations on feast days and fees for marriage, baptism and sanctuary, and bequests but installed a vicar who was paid a fixed lesser amount. The Hospitallers were responsible for the maintenance of the chancel (and provision of bread and wine for the Eucharist), and the parish of the nave. In 1338 these sources were worth at least £1,600 per annum, excluding the churches appropriated to Minchin Buckland. At Sutton St Michael in Herefordshire the average annual revenue for the church in the 14th century was £10; 20 shillings went to the stipend of the vicar with 6s 8d going on church expenses leaving £8 13s 4d for the Order.

In the Statutes of 1258-77 it was stated that some appropriated parishes lacked a priest and that steps should be taken to correct this position. In some cases where the revenues of the church were inadequate parish priests lived in a neighbouring commandery to save funds; Slebech maintained seven priests in 1338, six of whom served in local parishes.

Apart from Clerkenwell most of the commanderies were fairly simple buildings, their *raison d'etre* being in the main to superintend the gathering in of revenues deriving from agriculture. Many had hospices for the care of the poor and sick and accommodation for pilgrims.

The liturgy used in Hospitaller chapels and appropriated churches was based on that of the Holy Sepulchre in Jerusalem. In addition feast days observed in Rhodes (and briefly Malta) were followed in all the Order's European churches, and prayers were offered up in them for the Grand Master. The chief devotional cult was that of St John the Baptist.

The 'extent' of 1338 identified 42 commanderies, eight cameras (properties held in absentia without a resident commander), 34 knights, 34 chaplains, 48 servientes (sergeants) and four donati. In addition there were about 500 corrodaries (essentially pensioners), clerks, squires and servants. 70 chaplains assisted in appropriated churches. No mention is made of those resident in the Convent in Rhodes or the unprofessed. The English Knights Hospitaller seem to have been recruited from the gentry rather than the aristocracy. After the fall of the Templars the Knights Hospitaller were supposed to contribute 28 of the 200 Knights at that stage resident at the Convent in Rhodes. There is fairly clear evidence that the number of Knights fell during the later Middle Ages as some commanderies were grouped together under a single individual, and some leased.

The 'extent' is basically a record of income and expenditure, listing mansions, kitchen gardens, orchards, dovecotes, pastures, cattle, oxen, horses and 'confraria', a voluntary contribution from pious neighbours which in 1338 amounted to £888 4s. 3d. for all England. The Order had establishments in 26 English counties and Wales. Several of them with an income of £1000 per annum in the aggregate had been commanderies of the Templars. In 1338 the estates in England and Wales yielded £6,839 9s 9d; after expenses £3,826 4s 6d was sent to the treasury in Clerkenwell. £2,303 15s 2d was eventually sent to Rhodes as 'responsions'.

The following were the approximate annual revenues – in descending value – of the main commanderies in 1338:

Clerkenwell, London – £400
Slebech, Pembrokeshire – £307
Willoughton, Lincolnshire – £284
Carbrooke, Norfolk – £192
Shingay, Cambridgeshire – £187
Dinmore (& Garway), Herefordshire – £183
Quenington, Gloucestershire – £179
Temple Bruer, Lincolnshire – £177
Ribston, Yorkshire – £167

Halston, Shropshire – £157
Dalby, Leicestershire – £129
Buckland, Somerset – £125
Eagle, Lincolnshire – £122
Maltby-le-Marsh, Lincolnshire – £116
Chippenham, Cambridgeshire – £110
Melchbourne, Bedfordshire – £106
Templecombe, Somerset – £106
Fryer Mayne, Dorset – £96
Ossington, Nottinghamshire – £95
Yeaveley, Derbyshire – £95
Ansty, Wiltshire – £93
Battisford, Suffolk – £93
Swingfield, Kent – £87
Skirbeck, Lincolnshire – £84
Beverley, Yorkshire – £83
Dingley, Northamptonshire – £79
Grafton, Warwickshire – £78
Poling, Sussex – £78
Maplestead, Essex – £77
Greenham, Berkshire – £76
Trebigh, Cornwall – £75
Hogshaw, Buckinghamshire – £74
Hardwick, Bedfordshire – £69
Godsfield, Hampshire – £67
Clanfield, Oxfordshire – £60
Mount St John, Yorkshire – £58
Newland, Yorkshire – £56
Bodmiscombe, Devon – £50
Standon, Hertfordshire – £34
Chibburn, Northumberland – £24

(The importance of Lincolnshire with its five commanderies yielding a total annual revenue of £783 will be noted; the next most important county in terms of revenue (after Clerkenwell) was Yorkshire with its four commanderies yielding a total annual revenue of £364).

In the 14th century the Priory became more subordinated to the Crown and the Priors had unwillingly to take the oath of fealty to the relevant king. Communication with the Convent in Rhodes and the payment of 'responsions' became more difficult. Nevertheless the Hospitallers were exempted from the 'nationalisation' of alien priories and allowed to transmit bullion and men to Rhodes. Prior Robert Hales acted as Richard II's Admiral of the Western Fleet but then in 1380 became the King's Treasurer at the time the King had instituted a poll tax. Hales together with the Lord Chancellor, Archbishop Sudbury, became the object of the hatred of the mob during the Peasants' Revolt the next year. The Commandery at Clerkenwell was attacked and partially destroyed while Sudbury and Hales were seized from the Tower of London and beheaded on Tower Hill.

During the course of the 15th century the Prior of England had his title aggrandised to Grand Prior of England. It became increasingly difficult for Grand Priors to visit Rhodes; Grand Prior Botill for instance was refused permission by Henry VI in 1459. This may have accounted for Botill's support of Edward IV in 1460. For part of the period until his death in 1468 he had care of the Privy Seal.

Edward IV then tried unsuccessfully to impose his 20 year brother-in-law Richard Woodville as Grand Prior. However the Order managed to have the veteran Sir John Langstrother accepted as Grand Prior instead. The latter had, it transpired, deep Lancastrian loyalties and he commanded the centre of Henry VI's army at the Battle of Tewkesbury in 1471; after the Lancastrian defeat he was seized from the Abbey where he had sought sanctuary and executed on the orders of Edward IV.

Communal religious life outside Clerkenwell ceased during the 15th century and no other commandery is known to have had more than one brother in residence after 1460.

The Grand Prior managed increasingly to get control of individual commanderies for his own financial benefit; in 1440 it was agreed Grand Prior Robert Botill should be granted the small commanderies of Greenham, Hogshaw, Maltby, Poling and Skirbeck.

An interesting letter of c 1448 survives from Fra' Hugh Middleton, Turcopolier from 1442 in Rhodes, to his agent in England. He had been given the commanderies of Willoughton, Temple Bruer and Maltby (all in Lincolnshire) as his appanage. He is much concerned by various agricultural details and by non-receipt of certain moneys.

Sir John Weston became Grand Prior in 1477 and managed to maintain cordial relations with Edward IV, Richard III and Henry VII. The Grand Priory regained much of its prestige with the advent of the Tudors in 1485, although not its independence. The Turcopolier Sir John Kendal was elected Grand Prior in 1489 and continued in office until his death in 1501 when he was succeeded by Sir Thomas Docwra. The latter spent as much time acting as a royal servant as functioning as Grand Prior.

Two chaplains of the Order appear to have been appointed as suffragan bishops with titles *in partibus infidelium* – Thomas Cornish in 1480 to 'Tinen', who functioned in the dioceses of Bath & Wells and Exeter, and William Bachelor in 1515 to 'Carvaghazonen', who functioned in the diocese of Chichester.

The fall of Rhodes in 1522 (and the Grand Priory had sent more than £6,000 to assist in its defence) put pressure on both the English Langue and the Grand Priory of England. Henry VIII wished to nationalise the Grand Priory of England and use the Knights for the defence of Calais. A visit from the Master, de Lisle Adam, in 1528 was however able to prevent this scheme.

In 1527 Docwra died. His successor was Sir William Weston. The Act of Supremacy in 1532 was a particular problem for the Hospitallers with its abolition of the title and authority of the Pope within the realm; the collection of confraria was on the basis of papal authority.

In 1538 Henry VIII, by then Supreme Head of the Church and since 1511 (self-proclaimed) Protector of the Order, took control of the Grand Priory. He licenced the Grand Prior to receive English subjects into the Grand Priory provided they had taken the oath of allegiance. Brethren appointed to commanderies had to repudiate papal authority, and the first year's revenues went to the Crown.

In 1539 Fra' Thomas Dingley, Commander of Baddesley, and Sir Adrian Fortescue, a Knight of Honour, were beheaded for denying the Royal Supremacy. The latter was born in Hertfordshire. His mother was great aunt to Anne Boleyn. He served in France at the Battle of the Spurs in 1513 and was present at the Field of the Cloth of Gold seven years later. In 1532 he was admitted as a Knight of St John. The terms of the accusation were that he 'not onelie most trayterously refused his duty of allegiance which he ought to bear unto Your Highness but also committeth diverse and sundrie detestable and abominable treasons, and put sedition in your realm'. Then in 1541 another professed brother Fra' David Gunstone was hanged and quartered. Two more brethren died in prison. The Langue itself numbered less than fifty at the time, and therefore in percentage terms the Order gave more lives for the Papacy in England than any other order in England except for the Carthusians. The 17th century historian Fuller commented 'The Knights Hospitallers, being gentlemen and soldiers of ancient families and high spirits, would not be brought to present to Henry VIII such puling petitions and public recognitions of their errors as other Orders had done.'

In May 1540 the Langue of England itself finally fell victim to the greed of Henry VIII and was dissolved by statute in England as the brethren had 'sustained and maintained the usurped power of the Bishop of Rome'. The Grand Priory of England itself was dissolved in England in September of that year. The lands of the Grand Priory were confiscated. Pensions were awarded to the four Grand Crosses (The Grand Prior of England, the Prior of Ireland, the Turcopolier and the Bailiff of Eagle), 22 English Knights and four chaplains. Grand Prior Weston was awarded the very handsome pension of £1000 per annum but died on the actual day of dissolution. He was buried in the church at Clerkenwell. All the brethren in England save the five who were executed or died in prison as mentioned above in fact seemed to have acquiesced in the dissolution.

A small number of Catholic exiles kept the Langue of England going in Malta. The Turcopolier Sir Nicholas Upton, commanded the cavalry during the invasion of Malta by Dragut in 1551. He was a large, fat man and expired from the heat during the battle.

Queen Mary on her accession in 1553 immediately sent an agent to Malta to discuss the revival of the Grand Priory. The Grand Priory of England was then revived by Queen Mary in 1557 who instructed Cardinal Pole to return such property as had not been alienated. Thomas Tresham became Grand Prior and Richard Shelley Turcopolier. Ten commanderies (including Clerkenwell and Eagle) still remaining in the possession of the Crown were returned to the Grand Priory. Neither Tresham nor Shelley had been professed before but various Henrician Knights did rejoin the Grand Priory.

Left: Sir Adrian Fortescue portrayed in 19th c glass from Belmont Abbey in Herefordshire.
Below: Grand Prior Weston's effigy in the church at Clerkenwell.

Above: the effigy of Sir Thomas Tresham in All Hallows, Rushton, Northamptonshire.

Sir Thomas Tresham, who had succeeded his father as Lord of the Manor of Rushton in Northamptonshire, was knighted by Henry VIII. He was initially a supporter of the Duke of Northumberland under Edward VI but broke with the latter when he proclaimed his daughter-in-law Lady Jane Grey as Queen after the King's death. Tresham supported Mary and proclaimed her Queen at Northampton, becoming high in her favour. His wife was Anne Parr, a first cousin of Queen Catherine Parr, and his second a widow, Lettice, Lady Lee. On the death of the second he became a Knight of Justice of the Order of St John of Jerusalem. In his will before he became Grand Prior he recorded 'Our sovereign Lord and Lady King Philip and Queen Mary by the advice of the most reverend father in God Reginald Poole my lord cardinal's grace… have of their accustomed goodness vouchsafed to appoint me… to take uppon me the said religion and the office of the Lord Prior of St Johannes of Jerusalem in England.'

However Queen Mary died in 1558 and the Grand Priory was again broken up by Queen Elizabeth I in 1559. Tresham interestingly was allowed to retain his title of 'Lord Prior' and his ex officio membership of the House of Lords but died the same year. His bearded alabaster effigy is still to be found in All Hallows, Rushton, Northamptonshire, having been moved in the 18th century from the demolished church of St Peter, Rushton. He wears the long black mantle of the Order over his armour with a white cross on his breast. The effigy is probably by the sculptors Gabriel and Thomas Roiley, who were based in Burton-on-Trent. The chapel in which the effigy lies was seriously damaged by fire in 1963 with some injury to the monument. It was cleaned and restored at the joint cost of the British Association of the Sovereign Military Order of Malta and the Venerable Order of St John of Jerusalem, and an impressive service of commemoration was held on 9th October 1968 at which members of both Orders were present.

With the abolition of the Grand Priory in England a form of landholding which had existed for roughly four centuries had come to an abrupt and sad end. It is worth noting that former Templar possessions which were transferred to the Hospitallers belonged to the latter for longer than they had to the former. As previously mentioned, the Order of St John was almost certainly the largest ecclesiastical landlord at the Reformation. The Knights Hospitaller however left not a great deal behind them in architectural terms. Their commanderies were built in the main as agricultural revenue-raising centres and not much was spent on their adornment apart from Clerkenwell. Because of their vow of poverty elaborate monuments to individuals were not commissioned. The chief architectural link is the various churches appropriated to them although architectural glorification would have in the main been a matter for the parish rather than the Knights Hospitaller. The countryside is however littered with references to St John's wood, St John's pasture, St John's farm etc.

Various of the former Knights Hospitaller created under Mary suffered under Elizabeth. Sir Edward Waldegrave died in prison in 1563 as did Sir Thomas Mytton in 1583. Sir Marmaduke Bowes was hung, drawn and quartered in 1573 for sheltering Catholic priests.

Sir Thomas Tresham's Catholic grandson built the 'Triangular Lodge' at Rushton in honour of the Trinity and the Mass. Pevsner said 'It is no more or less than a profession of faith in stone.' He had been knighted by Queen Elizabeth at Kenilworth in 1576 but was reconciled to Catholicism by the Jesuits in 1580. He was heavily fined and spent fourteen years of the rest of his life either in prison or in forced residence at his house in Hoxton. He was married to a Throckmorton of Coughton in Warwickshire. His son Francis became involved in the Gunpowder Plot in 1605, was arrested and died in the Tower of London. The estate at Rushton was confiscated with the Treshams dying out on the death of his nephew.

Sir Richard Shelley, the Turcopolier, left England on the accession of Elizabeth in 1558. He received a pension from Philip II of Spain. He resigned as Turcopolier in 1561 and the office was left vacant until it was

The 'Triangular Lodge' at Rushton.

fused with the Grand Mastership in 1582. From 1569 until his death in 1589 he lived in Venice where he acted as an informer for Elizabeth. He was not however allowed to return to England as he wished. The Shelleys remained Catholic until the 18th century. The atheist poet was of the same family.

A diminishing number of English Knights continued to live and fight in Malta until the next century. Sir Oliver Starkey was the only Englishman at the Great Siege of Malta in 1565 where he acted as Lieutenant Turcopolier and Latin Secretary to Grand Master La Valette. Sir Andrew Wyse joined the Order in 1582 and was Grand Prior of England from 1593 until 1631. Sir Nicholas Fortescue became a Knight in 1638 and had dreams of restoring the Grand Priory of England until his death at the Battle of Marston Moor in 1644.

After the death of Sir Andrew Wyse in 1631 Italians tended to be appointed Grand Priors

Sir George Bowyer, Bt, shown presenting the Catholic Church in Abingdon to St Edmund.

of England. However. Henry FitzJames, the illegitimate son of James II, Jacobite Duke of Albermarle, also became titular Grand Prior in 1689 but resigned on his marriage in 1701. A succession of Jacobites and Italians occupied the office until it finally lapsed in 1806.

In England the Order was *de facto* revived in the 19th century on the initiative of the convert Sir George Bowyer, Bt, who became a Knight of Justice in 1858, although various other British subjects were received *in gremio religionis* before then. The Sisters of Mercy who ran the Hospital of St Elizabeth under Bowyer's patronage adopted the cross of Malta and their hospital developed into the Hospital of St John and Elizabeth, built on the pre-Reformation property of the Order in St John's Wood. The Church of St John of Jerusalem at the Hospital of St John and Elizabeth remains the conventual church of the Order of Malta in England.

In 1876 the convert 7th Earl of Granard (educated at Eton) became the first President of the British Association of the Sovereign Military Order of Malta. He was succeeded by the convert 5th Earl of Ashburnham (educated at Westminster) in 1889, who was succeeded in his turn by the convert 11th Lord North (educated at Eton and Christ Church) in 1913. It took some time for the British recusant families fully to appreciate the charms of the Order; the first "cradle Catholic" President was the 1st Viscount Fitzalan of Derwent KG (educated at The Oratory School) in 1932 after the death of Lord North.

A majority of Cardinal Archbishops of Westminster (Nicholas Wiseman (1850-65), Francis Bourne (1903-35), Arthur Hinsley (1935-43), Bernard Griffin(1943-56), William Godfrey (1956-63), Cormac Murphy O'Connor (2000-2009) and Vincent Nichols (2009-) have accepted the rank of Bailiff Grand Cross. Cardinal Henry Manning (1865-92) was very helpful when the Association was set up.

There have been many prominent clerical and lay members of the British Association since its foundation including a considerable

The Church of St John of Jerusalem, Hospital of St John and Elizabeth, St John's Wood.

number of Catholic converts such as the 9th Duke of Marlborough and Monsignor Ronald Knox.

The Prince Consort accepted the Grand Cross of Devotion in 1839 and Edward VII as Prince of Wales was made a Bailiff Grand Cross of Devotion in 1881. From the accession of William IV in 1830 until the death of Edward VII in 1910 Knights of Malta were allowed to appear at court wearing their formal uniform. This privilege was rescinded by George V and has not been restored.

The Sub-Priory of Blessed Adrian Fortescue was founded in 1972 with Lord Robert Crichton-Stuart as Regent. The subsequent Regents were Fra' Viscount Furness, Fra' Andrew Bertie (subsequently Grand Master 1998-2008), the Earl of Gainsborough and Fra' Matthew Festing. In 1993 the Grand Priory of England was revived, with Fra' Matthew Festing as Grand Prior, having been effectively in abeyance since 1558, despite the various titular Italian and Jacobite Grand Priors appointed subsequently. Fra' Matthew Festing was elected Grand Master in 2008 and was succeeded as Grand Prior by Fra' Freddie Crichton-Stuart, who died suddenly in 2011. He was then succeeded by Fra' Ian Scott as 57th Grand Prior of England.

GAZETTEER

ENGLAND, SCOTLAND
AND WALES

GREATER LONDON

CLERKENWELL

The Commandery in Clerkenwell appears to have been founded in the reign of King Stephen in 1144 by one Jordan de Bricet. It rapidly became the headquarters of the Order in England, and the residence of the Prior, who occupied private quarters in the close. In the 14th century the Prior received an allowance of 20 shillings a day when resident. In the later Middle Ages he was assigned a group of commanderies to provide his support. He was assisted in his administration by the provincial chapter which met once a year either at Clerkenwell or Melchbourne (Bedfordshire) on either the Feast of St Barnabas (11th June) or the Nativity of St John the Baptist (24th June). In 1417 the chapter at Clerkenwell consisted of the Prior, the Sub-Prior, a number of knights and five others. It seems that some kind of conventual life continued, uniquely, at Clerkenwell until the very end in 1540.

The Commandery in Clerkenwell had land throughout what is now Greater London, more north of the river than south - in the City and Westminster and at Cranford, Edgware (c250 acres), Friern (from Fra') Barnet, Hackney (where the Templars also had property; the Maltese Cross appears on the Arms of Hackney), Hampstead (formerly Templar, 130 acres), Hampton (840 acres including the site of Hampton Court, effectively alienated by Cardinal Wolsey and then Henry VIII), Harefield (380 acres), Harrow, Hendon (formerly Templar, 55 acres), Highbury, Islington (1650 acres), Kingsbury, Marylebone (360 acres), St John's Wood and Tottenham. The Commandery also had land in Buckinghamshire, Essex, Hertfordshire, Kent, Surrey and Worcestershire.

The financial affairs of the Order were in the hands of the Treasurer, an official who often played an important role in the affairs of the Kingdom as well as those of the Order as in the 13th century at least he had to provide safe custody for the treasure and the jewels of the King.

The only reasonably full description of Clerkenwell as a community is that we have is the "extent" written by the Prior Philip de Thame for the Master in 1338. The head of the house was the Commander, and he was assisted by the Sub-Prior. The other professed were the procurator generalis privilegiorum, a serviens who acted as general procurator, the claviger (cellarer) and a retired Commander

The Gatehouse to the Commandery, Clerkenwell, built by Thomas Docwra.

from Derbyshire. The Sub-Prior was responsible for the clergy who consisted of three professed chaplains, ten secular chaplains, a deacon and a sub-deacon. There were also many lay servants. At this period the income of Clerkenwell was c£400 per annum.

Clerkenwell was near enough the centre of affairs to receive many royal and other visits. In 1185 there was a meeting of magnates to consider the appeal of the Patriarch of Jerusalem for assistance. The excommunicate King John spent March 1212 there. Henry IV passed the fortnight before his coronation at Clerkenwell in 1399 and the Emperor Manuel II of Byzantium was entertained on a visit there in 1400.

Few traces of the buildings of the Commandery remain although they probably lay to the north of the present church. The buildings were surrounded by orchards, gardens and fishponds. The first church with a round nave, 20 metres across, was consecrated by Heraclius, the Patriarch of Jerusalem in 1185. In 1381 the priory was burnt and the fires continued for three days. The church was rebuilt as a rectangle towards the end of the 14th century, and during the 15th century. The great tower was completed while Thomas Docwra was Grand Prior (1502-27); John Stow remembered it as "a most curious peece of workmanshippe, grauen, guilt and inameled to the great beautifying of the Cittie, and passing all others I have seen." Docwra also built the great gatehouse which survives to this day.

The most touching medieval architectural survival is the 12th century crypt of the original church. Here also, as mentioned earlier, the tomb of Grand Prior Weston (obit 1540) can be found *(page 17)*. (The 16th century tomb of the Knight with a Maltese cross and the sleeping page

The 12th century crypt at Clerkenwell.

in fact came from Valladolid in the early 20th century.)

In 1546 Henry VIII granted the site of the Hospital to the Protestant John Dudley, Viscount Lisle, later Duke of Northumberland. Under Edward VI the nave of the church and the great tower were blown up to provide stone for the house the Duke of Somerset was building in the Strand. The buildings were however left to Princess Mary who

when she became Queen was able to restore them to the Order in 1557. Under Elizabeth these eventually ended up in the hands of William Cecil, Lord Burghley who bequeathed them to Lord Aylesbury.

The church subsequently became a Presbyterian meeting house.

In 1827 Sir Robert Peat, Chaplain Extraordinary to George IV, attempted to refound the Grand Priory of England with both Anglican and Catholic members but this exercise was rejected by Rome. In 1854 an independent non-Catholic brotherhood was set up and called "The Grand Priory in the British Realm of the Most Venerable Order of the Hospital of St John of Jerusalem". In 1888 Queen Victoria became the Priory's sovereign and since then a royal prince has always been Grand Prior. Edward VII was a great supporter. The present Grand Prior is the Duke of Gloucester. The Venerable Order acquired the old gatehouse and chapel at Clerkenwell in 1874 and made it its headquarters, which it remains to the present day. In 1931 the parish of St John of Jerusalem, Clerkenwell was merged with that of St James, Clerkenwell. The church of the former parish was deemed surplus to the requirements of the new parish and accordingly handed over to the Venerable Order. An excellent museum is maintained in the headquarters of the Venerable Order. It contains various remnants from the Commandery and Church at Clerkenwell including a boss of Abraham about to sacrifice Isaac.

CRANFORD

The advowson of the church of St Dunstan was given by John de Cranford to the Knights Templar from whom it passed after 1312 to the Hospitallers. However by 1363 the living seemed to be in the hands of Bishop Roger of Lichfield. In 1365 it passed to the Abbot and Convent of Thame. The estate was given in 1540 by Henry, Lord Windsor and eventually purchased by the Earls of Berkeley. The tower of the church is 15th century.

FRIERN BARNET

The church of St James was given to the

Top left: vaulting boss, the Sacrifice of Abraham, Clerkenwell.
Bottom left: St Dunstan's, Cranford.
Bottom right: St James Church, Friern Barnet

Above: St James Church, Friern Barnet

Above: St Mary's Church, Harefield

Below: St Augustine, Mare Street

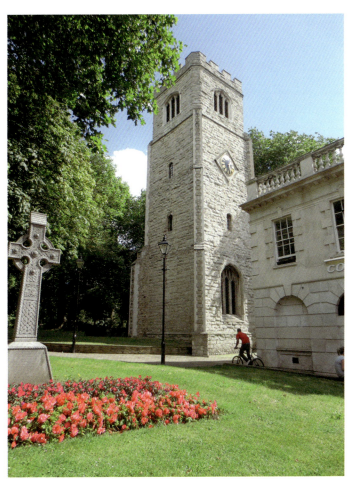

Hospitallers in 1187, together with the Manor of Whetstone. In 1544 the living was given to the Chapter of St Paul's. The old church provides the south aisle and the south door is 12th century. The interior is heavily restored. The church is now the Greek Orthodox church of St Katherine, having been leased from the Church of England.

HACKNEY

The church of St Augustine, Mare Street was built by the Knights Templar. The medieval tower survives. After their suppression the name of the church changed to St John.

HAREFIELD

The advowson of the church of St Mary was given to the Hospitallers by Beatrice

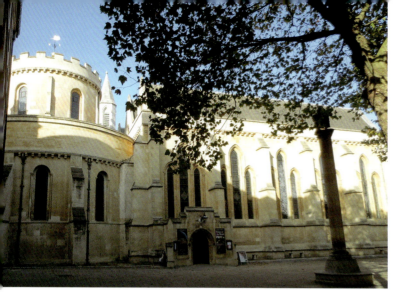

de Bollers in the late 12th century. The church was variously built between the 12th and the 16th centuries. (The wonderful monuments which are the chief claim to fame of the church date from the late 16th century onwards.)

THE TEMPLE

The site surrounding the Temple Church was acquired in the 1160s as the headquarters of the Templars in England. They had previously been, from the 1140s, at Old Temple at the northern end of Chancery Lane. The New Temple was a complex of buildings including a cellar, a storehouse, a kitchen, a stable, a brewery, a granary, a dormitory and the Master's Wardrobe. The buildings were surrounded by an orchard, a garden and pasture. The Temple was used with some regularity as a base for both monarchs and papal legates.

The round church which forms the nave was based on the round church in Jerusalem, the church of the Holy Sepulchre *(above, left and right)*. Building commenced in 1166; the church was devoted to the Virgin Mary. It is 18 metres in diameter and contains the earliest set of freestanding Purbeck marble columns in England *(below)*. The church was consecrated by Heraclius, Patriarch of Jerusalem, in 1185. The rectangular aisled chancel was built later in Early English style, and was consecrated on Ascension Day 1240 in the presence of Henry III *(opposite page)*. The earliest part of the church is the great west door, which is a seven-arched Norman doorway with dog-tooth decoration. *(Above right)*. There are nine stone effigies in the church, the most famous of which was of William Marshall, Earl of Pembroke, who died in 1219. Two of his sons are also buried there. The effigies are not of Templars themselves since like the Hospitallers they took a

vow of poverty which would have precluded effigies, but of illustrious supporters. The effigies all suffered in the Blitz *(opposite page)*.

After the Dissolution of the Templars the Temple area was immediately seized by the then Earl of Pembroke and Hugh le Despenser, favourites of Edward II, in spite of it being granted to the Hospitallers, who only recovered the ownership in 1340. By then the lawyers, that egregious breed, had inserted themselves into the Temple and received leases from the Hospitallers. They remain there some 675 years later.

WESTMINSTER

St Clement Danes, Strand was appropriated to the Templars in 1170 and eventually the advowson was obtained by the Hospitallers. The church was completely rebuilt by Sir Christopher Wren 1680-82

BEDFORDSHIRE

DEAN

The Church of All Saints was granted to the Hospitallers in the 12th century by Alice de Clermont, Countess of Pembroke. The south door is ancient. The chancel is 13th century, the tower and aisles 14th century. The angel roof and clerestorey is 15th century. There are good medieval wooden screens and a pulpit, and a brass of a priest called Thomas Parker obit 1501 with a scroll above bearing the words "Misere mei Deus secundum magnam misericordiam tuam".

KEMPSTON (HARDWICK)

The Commandery of Hardwick was founded at some stage before 1279 and probably dissolved before 1489. In 1338 it possessed 370 acres of pasture and other assets. At the Dissolution it became the property of Sir Richard Longe. No traces remain.

LANGFORD

The manor of Langford Rectory together with land, a mill and all rights of sac and soc, toll and theam were granted to the Prior of the Hospitallers by Simon de Wahull, son of Walter the Fleming and Sybil his wife in the first half of the 12th century. No traces of the manor remain. The advowson of

This page: The Church of All Saints, Dean; clockwise from left: the brass for Thomas Parker, the south door, exterior view, the nave and detail of the angel roof.

Above: St Andrew's Church, Langford, exterior and the nave, right.

the Church of St Andrew went with the manor. The church is Decorated (totally rebuilt by the Hospitallers) and constructed in brown cobbles although the chancel is Perpendicular. Some medieval stained glass fragments remain.

LITTLE STAUGHTON

The advowson of the Church of St Margaret was originally in the hands of the Templars and then transferred to the Hospitallers. The church is constructed of limestone and brown cobbles. The south bay arcade is c1300 but the rest Perpendicular. There is a 14th century tomb recess.

MELCHBOURNE

In the 12th century Alicia de Clermont, Countess of Pembroke gave the manor and the church to the Knights Hospitaller. The grant was confirmed by King John in 1199. It was an important commandery and in 1242 and 1328 Chapters of the Priory were held there. In 1338 the Commandery owned 633 acres of arable land and 60 acres of pasture. The Commandery was usually one of the five held by the (Grand) Prior, and it was in the hands of Grand Prior Weston in 1540. In the 16th century Leland wrote "Here is a right fair place of square stone standing much upon pillared vault of stone and there are goodly gardens orchards and ponds and a park thereby." At the Dissolution the property of the Commandery was worth £241 9s 10.5d. In 1549 it became the possession of the First Earl of Bedford. In 1557 Melchbourne became part of the revived Grand Priory but Elizabeth gave it back to the Second Earl of Bedford after her accession. In 1608 it was conveyed to Lord St John of Bletso. No traces remain of the Commandery but the site is believed to be encompassed by Melchbourne Park. St Mary Magdalene Church belonged to the Hospitallers as well but the present church is mainly an 18th century construction; the west tower is medieval.

Below left: the Church of St Margaret, Little Staughton. Below: St Mary Magdalene Church, Melchbourne.

GAZETTEER: BEDFORDSHIRE

Left: All Saints' Church, Riseley, and above, the angel above the south door.

Below: the Church of All Saints, Souldrop.

RISELEY

The advowson of All Saints Church was granted to the Knights Hospitaller by Alicia de Clermont. The oldest part is the 12th century south aisle. The chancel was rebuilt in the 13th century and there is a 14th century north chapel. The north aisle was rebuilt in the 15th century. An angel surmounts the south door.

SOULDROP

The Church of All Saints was appropriated to the Hospitallers by Alicia de Clermont, Countess of Pembroke. The tower and spire date from the second half of the 13th century but the rest of the church is Victorian.

OTHER

The Knights Hospitaller in 1540 had other properties in Bedfordshire including ones at Biggleswade (formerly Templar), Clifton (243 acres and a fishery), Edworth (79 acres), Eversholt, Flitwick, Gretteford, Harwand, Millbrook (formerly Templar), Northill, Pelling, Sandy (formerly Templar), Sharnbrook and Swonton (formerly Templar).

BERKSHIRE

BISHAM

In the reign of King Stephen Robert de Ferrers, Earl of Derby, granted the manor of Bisham to the Templars; the latter established a commandery there. In 1307 Edward II granted the manor to various individuals before it was claimed by Thomas, Earl of Lancaster. After his death in 1322 it was granted to more individuals, including briefly Queen Isabella, before in 1337 it ended up in the hands of the Earl of Salisbury who in that year founded a house of Austin Canons at Bisham. This was one of the Templar properties that the Hospitallers never obtained possession of. The Hobys obtained the property after the Dissolution and survived there as, in due course, baronets until the 18th century. Bisham Abbey as it is now called is now the National Sports Centre. The 13th century Commandery of the Templars now forms the centre of the "Abbey"; there is a particularly fine 13th century doorway. ("One of the best surviving English examples of their preceptories" (Pevsner)). The Templars had the advowson of the Church of All Saints from the 12th century until 1307; thereafter the advowson of the church seems to have gone to the Hospitallers

Above: Bisham Abbey
Right: the 13th century doorway of the Commandery
Below: The Church of All Saints, Bisham

at Clerkenwell. The tower certainly dates from the mid 12th century although much of the rest of the church is heavily Victorianised.

BLEWBURY

(now in Oxfordshire)

The advowson of the Church of St Michael the Archangel was granted to the Templars of Bisham by Thomas de Sandeford after 1229. After 1324 the Hospitallers took over the living. It seems likely that Grand Prior Weston granted it to Cardinal Wolsey for the support of Cardinal's College (subsequently Christ Church) in Oxford. In 1531 Henry VIII took control of the living. The church is built of brick and flint. Much of the nave and chancel are 13th century. The crossing of the late 12th century church is intact. The north transept has a 14th century

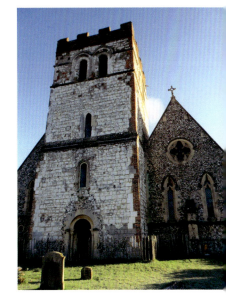

window and the tower is Perpendicular. There are stalls, an internal doorway, a font and various brasses.

BRIMPTON

Simon de Ovile, a tenant of William de Roumare, Earl of Lincoln, gave the manor of Shalford in the village to the Hospitallers by 1251. Edward I seems to have stayed here in 1302 as did Simon Gondavor, Bishop of Salisbury in 1314. In 1337 the Commandery was merged with that of Greenham. It possessed 360 acres of arable land and 25 acres of meadow. The manor passed to the Crown in 1540. At Brimpton Manor Farm can be found the derelict Hospitaller chapel of St Leonard. In the north wall there is a 11th century door with a tympanum on which can be found an engraved cross. The building is a flint rectangle and is mainly of the 12th century with north lancet and Decorated east window. The advowson of the Church of St Peter at Brimpton came to the Hospitallers in the 14th century but the building was completely rebuilt in 1869.

CATMORE

The advowson of the church lay with the Hospitallers from the reign of Richard I. The Church of St Margaret dates from the second half

Illustrations this page: The Church of St Michael the Archangel, Blewbury. Clockwise from above: exterior, nave and crossing, the font, brasses and the internal doorway.

Above: the derelict chapel of St Leonard at Brimpton, and right, detail of its engraved cross.

of the 12th century but has been much restored. The bowl of the font is 12th century.

EAST ILSLEY

The advowson of the Church of St Mary was confirmed in 1199 to the Hospitallers. The building was 12th century in origin. The chancel is 13th century and the tower 14th. There are single lancet windows. The bowl of the font is 12th century.

Below: the Church of St Margaret, Catmore.
Below right: The Church of St Mary, East Ilsley.

GREENHAM

The manor of Greenham was given to the Hospitallers by Maud, Countess of Clare during the reign of Henry II. A commandery was set up which, by 1337, had absorbed that of Brimpton. Greenham had 360 acres of arable land and 200 acres of pasture. It was appropriated to the use of the Grand Prior in 1445. The Commandery was suppressed in 1540 but returned to the revived Grand Priory by Queen Mary in 1557. It was finally dissolved by Queen Elizabeth. No traces remain.

Above: the 12th century font at Catmore.

SPEEN

The advowson of the Church of St Mary the Virgin was given to the Templars before 1219 by William the Marshal the Elder, Earl of Pembroke. The Hospitallers retained the advowson from 1312 until 1388, Pope Urban VI having granted the actual rectory to the Bishop of Salisbury some eight years earlier. The church was rebuilt in 1860 although the original chancel and nave became the north chapel and aisle. (The church possesses a remarkable memorial to the Margrave of Anspach by Canova.)

UFTON RICHARD

The advowson of the church of St John the Baptist was granted early on to the Hospitallers. In 1434-5 the parish was united with that of Ufton Robert. Ufton Richard became a chapel and a pension was paid to the Hospitallers. After the Reformation the chapel became two cottages which were not pulled down until 1886; the site is still marked by a fragment of the western wall.

The original chancel and nave of the Church of St Mary the Virgin, Speen.

WOOLHAMPTON

The manor of Woolhampton was presented to the Knights Hospitaller by Robert Fererer, Earl of Derby, in 1159. The advowson of the Church of St Peter belonged by 1291 to the Hospitallers, who retained it until the Dissolution. The church was rebuilt, the nave walls of the old church being encased in the new walls. In the chancel of the old church the following inscription could apparently be found round a blue slab "*Hic jacet Richardus de Herclond rector hujus loci conditur cancelli*" ("Here lies Richard Herclond rector of the parish founder of the chancel.")

The Knights Hospitaller in 1540 had little more additional land in Berkshire.

BRECONSHIRE

LLANFEUGAN

The advowson of the Church of St Meugan was given to the Hospitallers of Slebech by the Lord of Penkelly between 1175 and 1198. The church is medieval and has the remains of a painted rood screen.

BUCKINGHAM-SHIRE

ADDINGTON

The advowson of the Church of the Assumption of the Blessed Virgin was granted to the Hospitallers before 1220. The nave has 14th century arcades although the chancel is by Street in 1859. The tower was restored c 1490.

Above: the Church of St Meugan, Llanfeugan, exterior and interior and the remains of the Rood screen.

Below: the Church of the Assumption of the Blessed Virgin, Addington

BUCKINGHAM

St John's Hospital for the poor dates from the late 12th century. By the 13th century it was in the hands of Matthew de Stratton, Archbishop of Buckingham. He eventually granted it to the Master of St Thomas of Acon, London who converted it into a chapel and chantry. In 1289-90 he received a licence to transfer his property in Buckingham

Left and above: St John's Hospital, Buckingham

to the Knights Hospitaller; besides the hospital the land was assessed to amount to some 160 acres. At the Dissolution the chapel was dedicated to St John the Baptist and St Thomas of Acon. The 12th century chapel has a southern doorway and later medieval work. Until recently the Latin school, it now belongs to the National Trust.

BULSTRODE

The Templars had a commandery here in Gerards Cross by 1276. It was not initially acquired by the Hospitallers and in 1339 the King granted the manor and c130 acres to the Abbess and convent of Burnham. However in 1345 a judgement was given in favour of the Hospitallers who two years later leased out the land. No traces of the building remain. The possible site was at Moat Farm just north of the M40; part of the moat survives.

CHOLESBURY

The advowson of the church of St Lawrence seems to have passed to the Hospitallers in 1259. The church was rebuilt in 1872-3 and "cannot be called interesting" (Murray's Guide). The east window of the chancel and the piscina are 14th century and the south doorway 13th century.

CRESLOW

The advowson of the church belonged to the Templars and subsequently the Hospitallers. The church

Below: two views of the former church at Creslow.

38   THE KNIGHTS HOSPITALLER IN GREAT BRITAIN IN 1540

became derelict in the late 16th century with the last rector being appointed in 1554. The former church is to be found to the north west of the manor house (which never belonged to either order). It has had various incarnations since as a dovecote, a coach house and now a farm building. The north doorway is Norman in part, the windows Perpendicular and the roof 15th century.

EAST CLAYDON

The Hospitallers received the advowson of the Church of St Mary as late as c1500. The tower is late Perpendicular. Inside some Decorated work survives although the whole church was heavily restored by Street in 1871. Some medieval corbels survive.

HOGSHAW

The manor of Hogshaw (1.5 miles north of Quainton) was given to the Hospitallers in the reign of Henry II by William Peverel, and it became a commandery. They retained it until the Dissolution although after 1470 it was leased. The manor consisted of c350 acres and a dovecote. There are thought to be traces of the commandery at Fulbrook Farm and Doddershall Park. The church of St John Baptist was appropriated to the Hospitallers; it was ruinous by the end of the 17th

Above left: Cholesbury, the Church of St Lawrence.

Above and below: the Church of St Mary, East Claydon

LUDGERSHALL

The advowson of the Church of The Assumption of the Blessed Virgin was given to the Hospitallers by the mid 13th century. A church existed here in the 13th century. The chancel is 14th century while the nave was lengthened and aisles inserted fifty years later (both rebuilt by the Hospitallers). The interior is light and well proportioned. The piscina is 14th century and the tower 15th century. Angels line the wooden roof. There are two capitals of the 14th century arcades curiously carved with male heads. John Wyclif was appointed to the living by the Hospitallers in 1368.

Above: the medieval font from Hogshaw, now at Clerkenwell.

century. Part of the moat surrounding the church is reputed to survive, but now seems invisible. There are reputed to be beams from the church at Hogshaw Hill Farm. The medieval font of Hogshaw church can be found in the church at Clerkenwell.

Right: the Church of the Assumption of the Blessed Virgin, Ludgershall. Exterior and interior views, the carved capitals and angels on the wooden roof.

Left: Oving, the Church of All Saints.

OVING

The advowson of the Church of All Saints belonged to the Hospitallers as early as 1222 and remained with them until the Dissolution. The chancel is 13th century and the rest of the church is medieval although harshly restored in 1867. The font is 13th century. There is a wall painting with a seated figure of Christ.

QUAINTON

The advowson of the Church of St Mary the Virgin and Holy Cross belonged to the Commandery of Hogshaw until 1223 when Hervey Malet secured his claim to it against the Hospitallers. The church is essentially Victorian with no work surviving before the 14th century.

RADNAGE

The advowson of the Church of St Mary the Virgin was given to the Templars and after their dissolution passed to the Hospitallers. The church is backed by trees and in a sloping churchyard. The building dates from the early years of the 13th century. The piscina is 13th century. The font is Norman. The nave has a fine 15th century roof. Outside the south door can be found carved a double-barred cross, the use of which was granted to the Templars by Pope Eugenius III.

Below: Radnage, the double-barred cross by the South Door.

WIDMERE

There was a commandery of the Templars here (Great Marlow) from 1248 to 1338 with some 120 acres. At Widmere Farmhouse can be found a 13th to 14th century chapel with crypt.

The Knights Hospitaller in 1540 had other properties in Buckinghamshire including Calverton, Chalfont St Peter (formerly Templar), Hedgerley (formerly Templar), Quainton, Stony Stratford (formerly Templar) and Wycombe (formerly Templar).

Above: the Church of St Mary the Virgin at Radnage, exterior view, the 15th c roof and the Norman font.

Left: the old chapel at Widmere.

CAERNARVONSHIRE

PENMACHNO

The advowson of the Church of St Tudclud was granted to the Hospitallers. The church was originally 12th century. The present building was built in 1859. The font is Norman. The church was declared redundant in 1998 but was reopened in 2009.

CAMBRIDGESHIRE

CHIPPENHAM

The Hospitaller Commandery was founded by William de Mandeville, Earl of Essex in 1184 dedicated "to God and St Mary and St John the Baptist and the blessed poor of the house of the hospital of St John of Jerusalem and the brothers serving God in the same house.". It seems quite rapidly to have become the infirmary of the Order in England. Henry III was a frequent visitor. In 1338 the Order here possessed 660 acres, two dovecotes, two windmills etc; at this time the Commander and three brothers were based at Chippenham. In the 15th century the Commandery came under that of Carbrooke in Norfolk. There was a bad fire in 1446 after which many of the buildings were never rebuilt. After the Dissolution the Commandery was granted to Sir Edward North. The cellars of Lord Orford's School (now a private house) in the village may be be those of the Commandery. The church of St Margaret was never appropriated to the Hospitallers but belonged to the Abbey of Walden. The chapel of the north aisle however appears to have been maintained by the Hospitallers. There is a splendid wall painting there of St Christopher as well as others. A wall painting of St Michael weighing souls formerly bore the arms of Sir Robert Botyll, Grand Prior 1439-69.

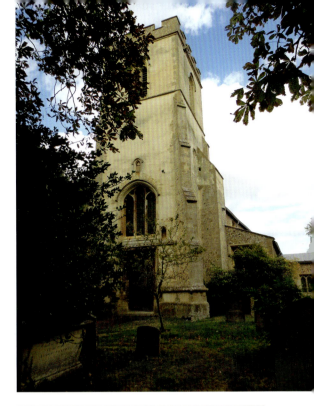

Right top: Chippenham, the Church of St Mary and St John the Baptist; below, Chippenham, wall paintings of Sts Christopher and Michael

DENNEY ABBEY

The "Abbey" was originally a priory of Ely Abbey and was set up in 1159. Ten years later the property was transferred to the Templars. Denney became an infirmary for sick members of the Order in the mid 13th century. 15 Templars were arrested here in 1308. After the destruction of the Templars the site was initially given to the Hospitallers who evinced little interest. In 1324 the Crown took the site back and three years later gave it to Marie de Chatillon, Countess of Pembroke. She had founded Pembroke College, Cambridge. She gave the abbey to the Franciscan Poor Clares. After the Dissolution the Abbey had various owners but eventually in 1928 became, appropriately, the possession of Pembroke College, Cambridge. There is evidence in the ruined church of Templar work. The west door dates from the later 12th century. The ruins are now looked after by English Heritage. There are also earthworks to the west of the abbey church, including fishponds.

DUXFORD

Before his death in 1230 William de Colville granted two carucates (c240 acres) and a mill to the Templars. A commandery was set up. After the suppression of the Templars the Hospitallers

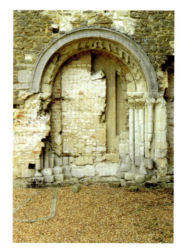

Above: Denney Abbey, views of the front and back; the 12th century west door, above left, and above, Templar work in the ruined church.

by 1333 had managed to obtain control of Temple Manor at Duxford with its 490 acres of land. It became a dependency of the Commandery at Shingay. Traces of a rectangular moat survive at Temple Farm between the farm and the river. The small chapel of St John the Baptist is sited some distance away by the crossing of the Icknield Way over the Cam. It appears originally to have been in the possession of the Templars. The chapel was rebuilt in 1337 as a chantry chapel. It is a rectangular building of flint rubble. There are four windows on both sides. As a chantry chapel it survived until 1548. It is now after various vicissitudes in the possession of English Heritage. The advowsons of the churches in the village were never in the hands of the Hospitallers.

EATON SOCON

The manor of "Eaton" was granted to the Hospitallers from at least 1218 and came under the Commandery of Melchbourne in Bedfordshire. The advowson of the church of St Mary the Virgin of Eaton Socon was given to the Hospitallers by the Beauchamps in the early 13th century. Most of the church seems to be early 15th century although some 14th century work survives.

Above and right: exterior and interior views of the Chapel of St John the Baptist at Duxford.

GREAT WILBRAHAM

In 1226 Peter Malaunay gave land to the Templars in the village. The Hospitallers obtained possession of some 770 acres in 1313 and remained there until 1540. The site is the 17th-18th manor house called Wilbraham Temple at Wilbraham End. By 1169 the monks of Ely had agreed to give the church of St Nicholas to the Templars. The Hospitallers obtained the advowson in 1313 and kept it until their suppression. The church was rebuilt to a cruciform Early English plan in the 13th century. A 12th century square font survives from the earlier building. Some medieval panelling (with more recent superstructure) survives, as do some floriated coffin lids.

Top left: St Mary the Virgin, East Socon.

Left and below: Church of St Nicholas, Great Wilbraham, exterior view, panelling, floriated coffin lids and the nave.

The font at Great Wilbraham.

Above and right: St Mary the Virgin at Sawston.

SAWSTON

Ralph Pirot is said to have pledged the advowson of the Church of St Mary the Virgin to the Hospitaller Commandery of Shingay as security for a loan of barley. On his failure to repay, the advowson passed to the Hospitallers. By 1278 the church was definitely appropriated to the Hospitallers. The church is of rubble with ashlar dressings. The nave is of the late 12th century and the chancel is of the 13th. The aisles were added in the 14th century. The Victorians restored the church heavily in the 1870s; it is now carpeted, with modern chairs. (The Huddlestons at Sawston Hall were, after the Dissolution, a famous recusant family).

SHINGAY

The manor was given before 1147 to the Hospitallers by Sibyl de Rames, daughter of the Earl of Shrewsbury, and her son-in-law, Robert, Earl of Gloucester. The Hospitallers founded a commandery here and this survived until 1540. The General Chapter met here in 1371. The site of the Commandery was south of the mill stream and north east of the later Manor Farm. The Hospitallers owned some 720 acres in the parish as well as two dovecotes, one water mill and one windmill. Lying near the old North Road the Commandery played host to royalty on a number of occasions. It was attacked during the Peasants' Revolt in 1381. Moat earthworks (visible from the air) surround the deserted village and Commandery. After the Conquest the church of St Mary at Shingay was appropriated to the Abbey of St Martin at Seez. By 1256 it had been appropriated by the Hospitallers. A church was built during the 15th century and the tomb of a Commander, Sir Robert

Above: the deserted site at Shingay.

Dalizon, who died in 1404, was apparently to be found there. The church became ruinous during the 17th century and Lord Orford replaced it 1697. This in its turn disappeared during the course of the 19th century. A local legend says that a ghostly coach is sometimes seen between the site of the Commandery and Shingay. This is possibly a memory from the reign of King John when Rome placed England under an interdict. Nobody could be baptised, married or buried except by the exempt religious orders such as the chaplains of the Knights Hospitaller. The "coach" could be a hearse.

WENDY

The Church of St Mary was transferred from the monks of Ely to the Templars by 1170. The Hospitallers gained the advowson after the suppression of the former and it was attached to the Commandery of Shingay. The medieval church was ruinous by 1734 and replaced by a new building. The latter became ruinous in its turn and replaced by a new building in 1866. This has now been demolished and again replaced.

The Knights Hospitaller in 1540 had various other lands in Cambridgeshire including those at Ashley cum Silverley (c 850 acres), Carlton (c180 acres), Gransden (50 acres) and Little Wilbraham (124 acres).

CARDIGANSHIRE

LLANRHYSTYD

The advowson of the Church of St Rhystyd was given to the Hospitallers of Slebech by Rhys ap Gruffyd before 1197. The church was rebuilt in 1852-4.

LLANSANTFFRAID

600 acres of land and the advowson of the Church of St Ffraed (anglice St Bridget) were given to the Hospitallers of Slebech by Roger, Earl of Clare between 1158 and 1164. The church was rebuilt in the 1840s. The font is 12th-13th century.

TROEDYRAUR

100 acres of land and the advowson of the Church of St Michael were granted to the Hospitallers of Slebech between 1158 and 1165 by Roger, Earl of Clare. The medieval church was demolished in 1795; the present church dates from 1850-1. There is a 14th-15th century font.

YSTRADMEURIG

The advowson of the Church of St John the Baptist was given to the Hospitallers of Slebech before 1158. The old church was demolished and completely rebuilt in 1898.

CARMARTHENSHIRE

CILMAENLLWYD

The advowson of the Church of St Philip and St James was given to the Hospitallers of Slebech before 1198. The church was completely rebuilt in 1843.

LLANSTEPHAN

170 acres and the advowson of the Church of St Ystyffan (St Stephen until the 1960s) was given to the Hospitallers of Slebech in the 1170s by Geoffrey de Marmion. The Normans rebuilt the church after 1112. The nave dates from the 13th century. The transepts were added in the mid to late 15th century.

The Knights Hospitaller in 1540 had various other properties at Carmarthenshire including one at Cilsant (120 acres).

Above: Llanstephan, the Church of St Ystyffan

CHESHIRE

The Knights Hospitaller had various properties in Cheshire including shares of salt pits.

CORNWALL

MADRON

The Church of St Madern at Madron was given to the Templar Commandery of Trebigh by a member of the Pomeroy family in the 12th century, and subsequently passed to the Hospitallers. The church is mainly 15th century with some good 14th century work visible in the chancel. The disused font is Norman. J.P.St Aubyn over restored the interior of the church in 1887. Outside can be seen an attractive niche and a cross, respectively above the south and the north doors.

Below: exterior views of the Church of St Madern at Madron.

ST CLEER

The advowson of the Church of St Clarus was given to the Templars and was taken over subsequently by the Hospitallers. The Norman church was enlarged towards the end of the 13th century. More additions were made in the 14th and 15th centuries. The old roofs have survived the restoration of 1870. The fine tower is Perpendicular. There is a good Norman font. Holy Well, north of the churchyard, is a pretty Breton-looking 15th century building.

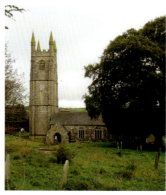

Above and above right: interior and exterior views of St Clarus at St Cleer. Right: Holy Well.

Below: St Ivo's Church at St Ive, exterior and and the roof and capitals inside

ST IVE

St Ive is between Callington and Liskeard and should not be confused with St Ives in the west. The church of St Ivo was appropriated to the Templars, subsequently the Hospitallers. The church is mainly 14th century with Perpendicular additions. The east window is good. It has a splendid roof with bosses and angels and interesting capitals. The church was restored in the 1880s.

TEMPLE, NR BLISLAND

The church of St Catherine was built at some stage by the Templars in the 12th century and became Hospitaller after 1312. The church was rebuilt during the last half of the 19th century, retaining the tower from the earlier building. The base of the Norman

font is preserved in the inner doorway. Modern glass commemorates the Templars. Various Templar/Hospitaller crosses remain on a building outside.

TREBIGH

Henry II gave the manor of Trebigh to the Templars after 1150. This was transferred without difficulty to the Hospitallers after 1312 and the Commandery became the centre of their Cornish estates. In the middle of the 15th century the Commandery was united with that of Ansty in Wiltshire. At the time of the Dissolution the land (200 acres) was leased. In due course the house became owned by the Wrey family. The lintel on the north west wall of the present farm has designs resembling Maltese crosses. There is apparently some evidence of Early English work inside.

The Knights Hospitaller in 1540 had little more additional land in Cornwall.

Above and left: the Church of St Catherine at Temple, exterior view, the modern stained glass and Templar crosses on the exterior of the building.

Below: details of the lintel at Trebigh.

CUMBRIA

The Knights Hospitaller in 1540 had various lands in Cumbria including 72 acres at Ireby. They also held the manor of Temple Sowerby which had originally been granted to the Templars in 1228.

DENBIGHSHIRE

YSBYTY IFAN (ALSO KNOWN AS DONGELWAL)

The Hospitallers set up a commandery here before 1195. It merged with Halston which maintained a hostel; no traces remain. They also had the advowson of the Church of St John, which was completely rebuilt by the Victorians.

DERBYSHIRE

BARROW-ON-TRENT

Barrow, situated on the north bank of the Rover Trent, was a camera of the Hospitallers with some 86 acres, a dovecote and a wind mill, which after 1433 came under the Commandery of Yeaveley. The church of St Wilfrid at Barrow-on-Trent was bestowed on the Hospitallers by Robert de Bagpuize during the reign of Henry II, and the land of the camera by his son. In 1526 a lease of Barrow was granted by the Grand Prior to one Ralph Pemberton. The land was given to Lord Mountjoy in 1543. Some remains of the camera were once thought (by Pevsner and others) to be found at Arleston House a mile to the north, which has certain modest remnants of medieval character; recent research seems to have disproved this. The Church of St Wilfrid is essentially 13th century. There is a 14th century alabaster effigy of a priest, possibly John de Belton obit 1349; next to it is a seemingly medieval graffiti of a Knight Hospitaller. There are various medieval cross slabs in the church and churchyard.

Right: St Wilfrid's, Barrow-on-Trent; exterior and interior views, the alabaster effigy of a priest and the graffiti of a Knight Hospitaller.

STANLEY

The advowson of the Church of St Andrew was given to the Hospitallers although only a moiety of the tithes were retained. The church is somewhat Victorianised; a Norman font survives.

STAVELEY

Half of the advowson of the Church of St John the Baptist was given to the Hospitallers during the second half of the 12th century by Hascoit Musard. The large church, submerged in 19th century industrialism, was originally 13th century. The upper part of the tower and south aisle are Perpendicular. There are a number of medieval brasses to the Frechevilles. High church fittings abound and the church is attached to Forward in Faith. A medieval Virgin and Child was found in the not too distant past in the rectory garden.

TEMPLE NORMANTON

Temple Normanton was granted to the Templars in the 12th century. It was never a commandery but came under the Templar structure in Lincolnshire. The estate seem to have amounted to some 300 acres. It passed after 1312 to the Hospitallers. There was a chapel dedicated to St Mary Magdalen. After 1540 the estate was briefly acquired by the Earl of Shrewsbury. No traces remain of manor or chapel.

TWYFORD

The Church of St Andrew was a chapelry of Barrow-on-Trent and its chaplain in the Middle Ages was appointed by the vicar of its mother church. The building is small and aisleless. A Georgian brick nave leads to a 14th century chancel through a Norman chancel arch with zigzag decoration. The lower section of the west tower has three Early English lancet windows. High up inside the tower can just be seen a Maltese cross. Legend

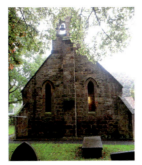

Top left: St Andrew's, Stanley, and right its Norman font.
Above: the Church of St John the Baptist at Staveley, and right, the medieval Virgin and Child.

has it that the Hospitallers offered a dole of bread and beer to pilgrims crossing the fords of the Trent (Twyford meaning "two fords") to the shrine of St Wystan (an 8th century Mercian saint) at Repton.

YEAVELEY

The Commandery of Yeaveley was situated one mile to the west of the village of that name at Stydd. During the reign of Richard I Ralph Foun, a tenant of the Meynells, gave land (108 acres and a dovecote in 1338) to the Hospitallers. In 1338 there was a conventual life at Yeaveley with three members of the Order and two corrodaries. This faded during the later Middle Ages. John Babington was Commander from 1509 to 1518; he subsequently became Grand Prior of Ireland and Turcopolier, dying in 1533. The land at Yeaveley was leased to Sir Thomas Babington in 1526. By 1535 Ambrose Cave was Commander which he remained until the Dissolution in 1540. In 1543 the land was given by Henry VIII to Lord Mountjoy. With the re-establishment of the Order in 1557 Henry Gerard briefly became Commander. The remains of the Commandery are hidden in a valley, approached by a muddy lane a mile off the A 515. A large moated platform supports a ruined wall of the chapel of St Mary and St John Baptist with 13th century lancet windows. The piscina from Stydd chapel can be found in the church of St Wilfrid, Barrow-on-Trent. The adjacent tall square 17th century brick hall with 19th century Gothick windows is now a farm house. "A remote and altogether mysterious place" (Henry Thorold, the Derbyshire *Shell Guide*).

The Knights Hospitaller in 1540 had various other properties in Derbyshire including ones at Brampton (formerly Templar, some 300 acres) and Tansley (100 acres).

Top: St Andrew's, Twyford; its Norman chancel arch and the Maltese cross in the tower.

Right: Yeavely, the ruined lancet windows, remains of the chapel of St Mary and St John Baptist.

Below right: the piscina from Stydd chapel now at Barrow-on-Trent.

DEVON

BODMISCOMBE

The Hospitallers acquired land in Bodmiscombe in Ufculme parish and set up a small commandery there. Some 300 acres of land were held there and at Cove. A court with gardens, woods and a dovecote existed. It appears to have closed as a commandery during the course of the 15th century and been taken over by Buckland in Somerset. By 1501 it was leased to the Vernay family. No traces remain.

BRENDON

The Church of St Brendan was originally granted to the Templars in the second half of the 12th century by Henry de Pomeroy before being transferred to the Hospitallers after 1312. It was substantially rebuilt in the 1730s. A memorable 12th century carved font survives.

CLAYHANGER

The manor was given by Hugh de Perepont to the Templars in the 12th century. The Hospitallers did not succeed in getting hold of the lands in the 14th century although they did fairly quickly acquire the advowson of the Church of St Peter. The east window is 14th century. The fluted font is c1200. There are no remains of the manor.

Top: the Church of St Peter, Clayhanger, and above, its fluted font.

Above left: the 12th century font at St Brendan's Church, Brendon.

GAZETTEER: DEVON

HALWILL

The Church of St Peter and St James was appropriated to the Hospitallers of Bodmiscombe. The tower with short pinnacles is medieval but the rest of the church was heavily restored in the 1870s.

TEMPLETON

The manor was originally Templar and transferred with the advowson of the church of St Margaret to the Hospitallers in 1312. The Shell Guide talks of a "lost and decrepit village in wildest Devon standing on a ridge between deep valleys". No traces of the manor remain. The advowson of the church seems to have been transferred to the Prioress of Cannington by 1362. The tower is probably 13th century.

The Knights Hospitaller in 1540 had various other properties in Devon including ones at Cruwys Morchard, Hele and Up Ottery (220 acres).

Top: St Peter and St James, Halwill, and below St Margaret's Church, Templeton.

DORSET

CHILCOMBE

An ancient camera of the Hospitallers existed here and possessed some 150 acres of land. It seems to have been leased out from the early 14th century. The revenue went to the nunnery of Minchin Buckland in Somerset. No traces remain.

FRYER MAYNE

A Hospitaller commandery was founded at Broadmayne before 1275 and merged with Baddesley (Hampshire) in 1471. It possessed some 355 acres. From 1533 the land was leased. The land was returned briefly to the Order in 1557. Few traces of the Commandery remain.

STINSFORD

The advowson of the Church of St Michael was certainly in the hands of the Hospitallers by 1338. The church is essentially 13th century although the tower is 14th. It was heavily restored in 1883. The chancel arch is richly moulded. There is a Norman font and an early carving of an angel. (Stinsford is Hardy's Mellstock in "Under the Greenwood Tree"; the author's heart is buried in the churchyard.)

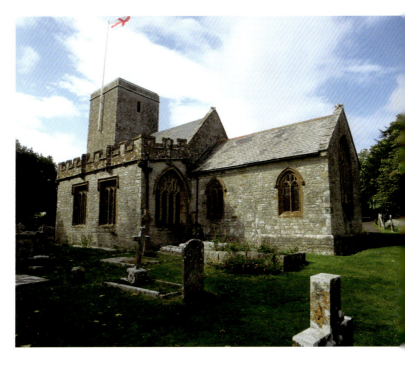

The Church of St Michael at Stinsford: top, exterior view; above, carved capitals, and above right the Norman font. Right: the carving of an angel.

GAZETTEER: DORSET

TOLLER FRATRUM

The manor with some 150 acres was given to the Hospitallers ("Fratrum" obviously meaning "of the brothers") in the 12th century. There may earlier have been a nunnery attached. In 1540 it was purchased by one John Samways. The site of the manor is probably that of Little Toller Farm. The little rustic Church of St Basil (there are only three dedications in England to that saint) was appropriated to the Hospitallers and survives. It was heavily restored in the 19th century. It closed for regular Anglican worship in 2010 and is now owned by a trust. It possesses two fittings of note - the Norman font with its remarkable carvings of humans and beasts and and a fragment of a stone relief of 1130 of St Mary Magdalene washing the feet of Christ.

OTHER

The Knights Hospitaller in 1540 had various other properties in Dorset including ones at Bloxworth, Buckland Newton, Charborough, Child Okeford, Dorchester, East Stafford, Fifehead, Frampton, Horton, Kingston, Knighton West, Langdon, Loders, Mappowder, Pilsdown, Sherborne, Swanage, Tarrant Gunville, Toller Porcorum, Waddon, Ware, Warmwell, Waye (160 acres) and Westbrook.

The Church of St Basil at Toller Fratrum, with its Norman font and the carving of St Mary Magdalene washing the feet of Christ.

(COUNTY) DURHAM

The Knights Hospitaller in 1540 had various properties in County Durham including one at Sedgefield.

ESSEX

BROXTED (ALSO KNOWN AS CHAWRETH)

The advowson of the Church of St Mary was granted to the Knights Hospitaller. "Thin 13th century lancets light (the) cold white interior". (Norman Scarfe - Essex *Shell Guide*.) The church is of flint and pebble rubble. There is a modern window of a Hospitaller. A modern kneeler reflects the Hospitaller past.

St Mary at Broxted: exterior view, and the lancet windows (right); below; the modern stained glass window, and above right the Hospitaller kneeler.

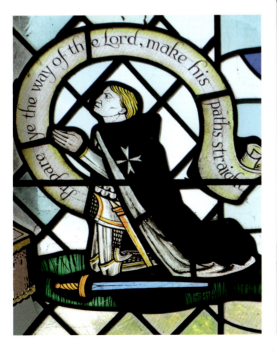

CRESSING TEMPLE

The manor of Cressing was granted to the Templars by Maud, Queen to King Stephen, by a charter issued in Evreux in 1136 for the benefit of the souls of her father, her husband and herself. King Stephen added the town of Witham in 1147-8. The Commandery was one of the earliest possessions of the Templars in England. It was transferred to the Hospitallers after 1312 and in 1337 possessed more than 1400 acres of land. Cressing Temple was attacked during the Peasants' Revolt in 1381. In 1515 the land was leased. At the Dissolution the lands were granted to Sir William Huse and John Smyth, a baron of the Exchequer. The site was purchased by Essex County Council in 1987. The Barley Barn (1220) and the Wheat Barn (1280) are among the among the finest such barns in Europe. The Templars (and subsequently) Hospitallers also held the advowson of the Church of All Saints, Cressing. The flint rubble church with its spire was built at various times between the 13th and 15th centuries.

LITTLE MAPLESTEAD

The village and church of Little Maplestead were given to the Hospitallers in 1185 by Juliana Fitz-Audelin. The possessions of the Commandery were extensive and land was owned in both Maplesteads, Gestingthorpe, Hedingham, Colchester etc. totalling at least 550 acres. By 1463 the Knights had ceased to live at the Commandery for it was then leased to one John Syday. Henry VIII granted the

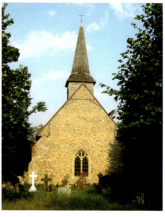

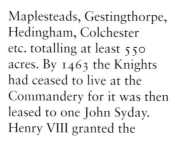

Cressing Temple. Top: the Wheat Barn; below, the Barley Barn and above left the interior of the Barley Barn.

Above: the Church of All Saints, Cressing.

manor to a certain George Harper in 1541. No traces of the domestic buildings remain. The flint Church of St John the Baptist at Little Maplestead does however survive. It is one of the four medieval round churches surviving in England and was built in 1337 to replace an earlier structure of 1241-5. The west end with its arcade of six elegant pointed arches is round leading up to an aisleless roofed chancel. The west doorway with its fleurons is 14th century. The church was heavily restored in 1851-57 by R.C.Carpenter. The font is Norman of c1080. The Venerable Order acquired the living of Little Maplestead in 1910.

STEBBING

The advowson of the Church of St Mary the Virgin was granted to the Hospitallers of Little Maplestead. The church was entirely rebuilt under the Hospitallers. Norman Scarfe in the Essex *Shell Guide* talks of "the distinguished and beautiful 14th century church." The chief excitement of the church is the 14th century stone screen, much restored by Woodyer. Fragments of medieval glass remain.

TEMPLE ROYDON

The manor of Temple Roydon was granted to the Knights Templar in 1198

by Robert Fitzwalter (obit 1235). In 1313 the Knights Hospitaller gained control of the manor. In 1540 the manor was granted to John Morice but in 1548 it became the possession of Princess Mary, who granted it to the revived Hospitallers in 1557. It subsequently became the possession of Lord Norris, then the Earl of Salisbury and eventually of Winchester College. Temple Farm may have the range of the medieval hall. In 1254 the Templars appropriated the rectory and installed a vicar; the

Little Maplestead: top, the Church of St John the Baptist; below, arcade of pointed arches, and the chancel roof. Below: the Norman font.

GAZETTEER: ESSEX

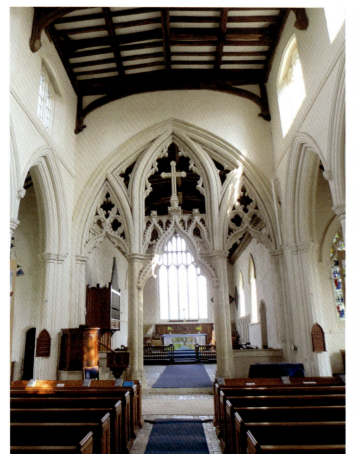

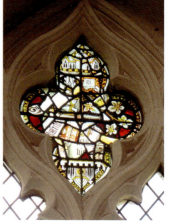

St Mary the Virgin, Stebbing; exterior views, the 14th century screen and remaining medieval stained glass.

Hospitallers retained the advowson. The church is flint and rubble with ashlar dressings. The church has a chancel and nave with north aisle and a western tower topped by a weathervane. The walls are 13th century and a lancet window survives. The font is medieval.

WEST THURROCK

Nothing remains of the manor. The Church of St Clement's, West Thurrock was originally appropriated to the Templars before belonging to the Hospitallers. It now has the rather dramatic background of the Procter & Gamble detergent factory. There is evidence of an earlier circular nave. The tower is 15th century, most of the rest of the building 13th. There is a half effigy of a priest of 1315 inside the church.

The Knights Hospitaller in 1540 had various other properties in Essex including ones at Bradwell (formerly Templar), Carlton (180 acres), Chingford (467 acres, formerly Templar), Finchingfield (formerly Templar), Foulness (formerly Templar), Fryerning, Great Maplestead, Havengrove Island (formerly Templar), Prittlewell (formerly Templar), Rainham, Rivenhall (formerly Templar), Rochford (formerly Templar), Sutton (865 acres, formerly Templar) and Terling (formerly Templar).

Top: Temple Roydon, exterior view, and views of the western tower and nave roof. The medieval font is shown above right.

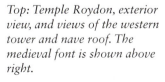

Above: St Clement's, West Thurrock, and right, the traces of the circular nave.

GAZETTEER: ESSEX

GLAMORGANSHIRE

CHERITON

The advowson of the Church of St Cadoc was given to the Hospitallers of Slebech by William de Turberville c 1165. The church was built in the early 14th century although there is an earlier Norman font.

ILSTON

The advowson of the Church of St Illtyd was given to the Hospitallers of Slebech between 1220 and 1232. The church is mainly 13th century although heavily restored in 1832.

LLANMADOC

The advowson of the Church of St Madoc together with the water mill and land was given to the Templars of Garway around 1156 by Margaret, Countess of Warwick. It passed subsequently to the Hospitallers of Dinmore. The chancel arch is 12th century and the rest of the church was rebuilt in the 13th century. There is a Norman font.

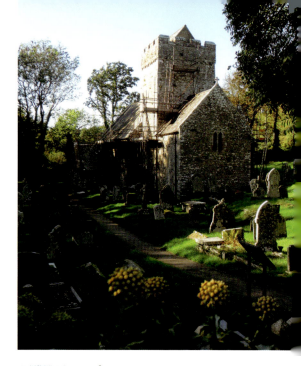

Clockwise from the top: Cheriton, the Church of St Cadoc; Ilston, the Church of St Illtyd; Llanmadoc, the Church of St Madoc, exterior and interior views.

LLANRHIDIAN

The advowson of the Church of St Rhidian and St Illtyd was given to the Hospitallers of Slebech by William de Turberville c 1167. The tower and the chancel are 13th century but the nave was rebuilt by the Victorians. In the church there is a mysterious "leper stone" with representations of human and animal figures, probably dating from the 12th century.

LOUGHOR

The advowson of the Church of St Michael was given to the Hospitallers of Slebech by Henry de Newburgh between 1156 and 1184. The church was completely rebuilt in 1885.

PENMAEN

The advowson of the Church of St John the Baptist was given to the Hospitallers of Slebech between 1198 and 1241. The church was completely rebuilt by the Victorians.

PENRICE

The advowson of the Church of St Andrew was given to the Hospitallers of Slebech c 1200 by John of Penrice. The nave and chancel of the church are 12th century.

PORT EYNON

The advowson of the Church of St Cattwg was given to the Hospitallers of

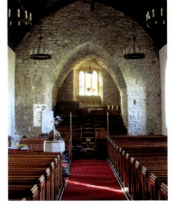

Above: Sts Rhydian and Illtyd at Llanrhidian, exterior view; right, the nave, and below, the "leper stone".

Penrice: above, the Church of St Andrew, and right, detail of the exterior.

GAZETTEER: GLAMORGANSHIRE

Slebech by Robert de Mare c 1165. The 12th century church was substantially rebuilt in the 1860s.

RHOSSILI

The advowson of the Church of St Mary the Virgin was given to the Hospitallers of Slebech by William de Turberville c 1165. The church is early 13th century with a splendid Norman doorway. The font is Norman.

The Knights Hospitaller in 1540 had various other properties in Glamorganshire including a Hospital of St John in Swansea (no traces remain).

Top: St Catwgg, Port Eynon. Below: St Mary the Virgin at Rhossili, with details of the Norman doorway, carved capital, nave and Norman font.

THE KNIGHTS HOSPITALLER IN GREAT BRITAIN IN 1540

GLOUCESTERSHIRE

DOWN AMPNEY

The cruciform Church of All Saints was built by the Templars around 1265 and in due course transferred to the Hospitallers of Quenington. The spire of the church is 14th century. There is a splendid effigy of Sir Nicholas de Valers (obit 1315) who was associated with building the church, and medieval red flower decoration. The church was severely restored in 1863 by Benjamin Ferrey. There are a number of external crosses on the building. (Ralph Vaughan Williams was born in the Vicarage at Down Ampney, whose name he used for the hymn tune for "Come down, O love divine".)

Down Ampney: above right, the Church of All Saints, the effigy of Sir Nicholas de Valers, and right, the medieval red flower decoration and altar.

GUITING POWER (ALSO KNOWN AS LOWER GUITING)

The Church of St Michael and All Angels was appropriated to the Templars, and subsequently the Hospitallers. Only the north and south doorways and the chancel survive from the 12th century. The tower and the font are 15th century.

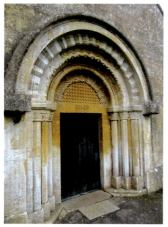

Above, Guiting Power, the Church of St Michael and All Angels, with views of the south doorway and the font.

Below: St Mary's Meysey Hampton; right, one of the lancet windows at Meysey Hampton.

THE KNIGHTS HOSPITALLER IN GREAT BRITAIN IN 1540

The Church of St Mary, Meysey Hampton; left, interior view, and above, the medieval glass fragment.

MEYSEY HAMPTON

The cruciform Church of St Mary was built by the Templars and dedicated in 1269. The east window is Decorated. The church was restored by Brooks in 1874. There is a remarkable fragment of medieval glass showing the Crucifixion with a green cross and red background.

QUENINGTON

The Manor of Quenington was given to the Hospitallers by Agnes de Lucy and her daughter Sibilla in about 1193, and a commandery was then established. It took over the Templar possessions of Templar Guiting after 1312 and possessed some 644 acres. The Commandery was surrendered to the Crown in 1540. It was granted back to the Grand Priory in 1557. The buildings were demolished by the 17th

Right: Quenington, the Gatehouse, and above, the Dovecot

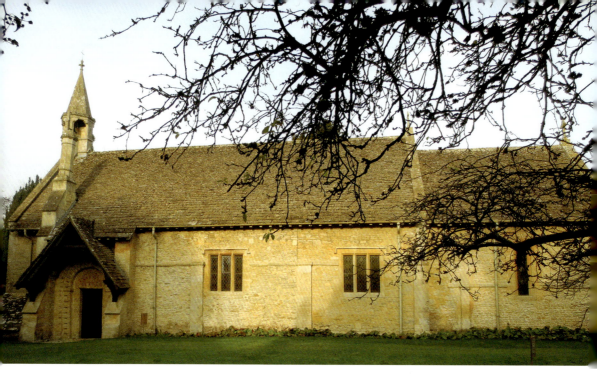

Quenington: top, St Swithin's Church, and above, the Harrowing of Hell, detail from the north door; and right, the south door, showing the Coronation of the Virgin.

century and Quenington Court was built on the site. Both a 14th century dovecote and and a 14th century gatehouse survive. The church (originally St Mary's but St Swithin's by the 18th century) was secured to the Hospitallers by the mid 12th century although they continued to pay a pension to St Peter's Abbey, Gloucester Abbey (now Gloucester Cathedral). The lower walls of the chancel and the nave are 12th century. The chancel windows are 13th and 15th century. The great glories of the church are the north and south doorways, the former showing the Harrowing of Hell on the tympanum and the latter the Coronation of the Virgin; these predate the arrival of the Hospitallers.

SIDDINGTON

The manor and the church of St Peter was given to the Hospitallers of Quenington around 1200. Of the manor a medieval tithe barn at Church Farm survives. The church is in the main of around 1200 with nave and chancel. The south doorway is Norman with a carving of Christ in Majesty on the tympanum. There is a Perpendicular chapel of c1470.

SOUTHROP

The church of St Peter was appropriated to the Hospitallers at Quenington

Siddington: top, the Tithe Barn, above, the Church of St Peter and right, the south door.

in the 13th century. It is built of limestone rubble with ashlar dressings. The nave is 12th century and the chancel, rebuilt by the Hospitallers, 13th. There are three aumbries and two piscina in the chancel. The treasure of the church is the 12th century font showing the Virtues overcoming the Vices. (John Keble was curate here 1823-5.)

TEMPLE GUITING

The Commandery of the Templars at Guiting was founded about the middle of the 12th century. Gilbert de Lacy, Roger de Waterville, Roger, Earl of Hereford and Roger d'Oilly were among the original benefactors. It had some 1,460 acres. The Crown seized the Commandery after 1308 but it was transferred in due course to the Hospitallers, who did not, however themselves maintain a commandery there. There is a late 16th century house (Manor Farm) on the site of the earlier Commandery. The church of St Mary was founded c1170. The chancel with its remarkable external

Southrop: above left, the Church of St Peter; above right, a doorway.

Left: the 12th century font showing the Virtues overcoming the Vices.

Temple Guiting, the Church of St Mary. Right, one of the three panels of 16th century stained glass, and below, two views of the exterior corbels.

corbels dates from the 12th century; one has a Templar cross on it. The rest of the church was rebuilt in the 18th century. There is a beautiful 15th century font and three panels of 1500 stained glass in the nave south window; the other nine panels are in the Metropolitan Museum of Art in New York.

OTHER

The Knights Hospitaller in 1540 had various other properties in Gloucestershire including ones at Atherley, Broughton (formerly Templar), Calmsden, Cirencester, Duntisbourne, Easthrop, Ferncote, Freshdene, Gloucester, Hampden, Ingiston, Nibley, Sandhurst, Twigworth, Westrop, Winstone, Wishanger (formerly Templar) and Yate.

HAMPSHIRE

FORDINGBRIDGE

The Church of St Mary is mainly Early English. It has an extra-parochial 13th century north chapel which belonged to the Templars and then the Hospitallers. The 15th century timber roof of the chapel is of considerable beauty. Outside is an altar tomb where the Templars were reputed to have sharpened their swords. The Templars may have had a commandery here but this has completely vanished.

GODSFIELD

Various grants were made by the Daundelys, Lords of Chilton Candover, to the Hospitallers during the 12th and 13th centuries. The first of these was made in 1171 in the presence of Henry of Blois, Bishop of Winchester. The Hospitallers established a commandery at Godsfield. In 1338 it held 300 acres. In 1365 the Commandery moved to North Baddesley. A chapel of flint and stone was built in 1360-70 and this still survives, in private hands, with its three lancet windows. A brick fireplace has been inserted where the altar once stood and no medieval fittings survive. In a 16th century survey "the fair chapell" was described

Below: Godsfield, the old chapel.

Above: Fordingbridge, The Church of St Mary, exterior, the nave timber roof and the altar tomb reputedly used by the Templars to sharpen their swords.

North Baddesley: the Church of St John the Baptist. Exterior and interior views, the raised tomb and details of the Hospitaller crosses.

as adjoining "a dwelling house for a gentleman builded with tymber with viij or nyne good lodging chambers....watered with a well of excellent good water with garden, orchard, barnes, stables and all other outhousing of all sortes sufficient". Remarkably the Godsfield pyx has survived. It was found in a hedge in the 1870s and is now to be found in the V&A. It dates from the 14th century and is engraved with acanthus foliage.

NORTH BADDESLEY

The manor of North Baddesley belonged to Ralph de Mortimer at the time of Domesday Book but at some stage before 1167 was alienated to the Hospitallers. In 1338 it possessed over 500 acres and a dovecot. It was initially a camera of Godsfield but in 1365 the Commandery migrated to North Baddesley. Three Commanders became Grand Prior including Sir William Weston at the Dissolution. The Commander at this time was Sir Thomas Dingley who was executed in 1539. The Commandery was dissolved in 1540 but granted back to the Hospitallers in 1557 with Sir George Aylmer as Commander. The 16th-18th century Baddesley Manor is on the site of the Commandery. The Hospitallers held the advowson of the Church of St John the Baptist (previously All Saints) - "A delightful building, set on a hillbrow with a view over miles of mainly wooded country" (Pevsner). The small nave is 14th century and the chancel 15th. The church has a pleasant High Church interior but is no longer used for regular worship. A raised tomb is set against the north wall of the chancel. It is decorated with Hospitaller crosses but the identity of the occupant (probably not an actual Hospitaller) is unknown. The church was restored by John Oldrid Scott or his brother. The Hospitallers also held 80 acres of land at nearby Rownhams.

TEMPLE SOUTHINGTON

The Templars had the manor and a commandery by 1240. In 1250 some of the land was sold to the Prior of Selborne for £200 "to buy other lands in aid of the Holy Land". After the suppression of the Templars the manor seems to have been seized by the Earl of Hereford but it eventually passed to the Hospitallers who did not set up a commandery but leased the land. No traces remain.

The Knights Hospitaller in 1540 had various other properties in Hampshire.

HEREFORDSHIRE

ACONBURY

In 1216 Margaret de Lacy founded a priory of sisters of the Order of St John of Jerusalem, with a hospital attached. By 1237 she had fallen out with the Order and transferred the convent with papal approval to the Augustinian canonesses. No traces of the convent remain. The church of St John the Baptist was built 1230-40. It is of rubble with red ashlar dressings. The style is Early English. Wooden angels adorn the western porch. The church is now the store for the Diocese of Hereford.

BOSBURY

The Templars had a commandery here at Upleadon known as Temple Court founded in 1217-19 by William Marshal, Earl of Pembroke. The commander in 1312 was Thomas de Tholouse who was arrested and put in the Tower of London although later released. The property of 780 acres was transferred to the Hospitallers at Dinmore. The only remnant is the course of a moat at Temple Court. There is a tomb slab with a foliated cross in the Church of Holy Trinity (of which they did not have the advowson) which could be for either a Templar or a Hospitaller.

BOULSTONE

The Hospitallers had the manor and the advowson of the Church of St John of Jerusalem. The church was largely rebuilt in 1876-7 by William E. Martin. The chancel south window is 14th century. It is now disused and functions as some kind of games room.

BRAMPTON BRYAN

The advowson of the Church of St Barnabas, Brampton Bryan was granted to the Hospitallers of Dinmore. The church was largely destroyed in the Civil War

Top: Aconbury, the Church of St John the Baptist, and below, one of the wooden angels from the porch.

Bosbury: the tomb slab in Holy Trinity Church.

Top: the disused Church of St John of Jerusalem at Boulstone.

Above: Brampton Bryan, the 14th century effigy of Margaret de Brampton.

Below: Dewsall, the Church of St Michael.

and was rebuilt by Sir Robert Harley in 1656. A 14th century effigy of Margaret de Brampton survives. (There is also a memorial to Robert Harley (1661-1724), First Minister to Queen Anne, who was created First Earl of Oxford and Mortimer.)

CALLOW

The Hospitallers had some 240 acres of land in the parish. The advowson of the Church of St Mary was also granted to the Hospitallers. The church was totally rebuilt c 1830.

DEWSALL

The advowson of the Church of St Michael was given the Hospitallers. The church is 13th-14th century.

DINMORE

A Hospitaller commandery was set up here before 1189 with some 400 acres. It was a major administrative centre for many properties and farms, and probably in 1540 third or fourth in importance in the country. The field names on the tithe maps disclose the long association of Dinmore with the Order – Friars Grove, Great St John's Meadow etc. The site of the Commandery is now that of the privately owned 16th-18th century Dinmore Manor, high up on a hill. Dinmore had a number of distinguished Commanders: Thomas de Burley (Prior of Ireland 1365), William Poole (Bailiff of Eagle 1433), Sir William Dawnay (Turcopolier 1449), Sir John Weston (Grand Prior of England 1476), Sir

GAZETTEER: HEREFORDSHIRE

Thomas Docwra (Grand Prior of England 1501), Sir John Buck (Turcopolier 1522) and Sir John Rawson (Prior of Ireland, created Lord Clontarf in 1541). Dinmore was granted to Sir Thomas Palmer in 1540. The only medieval architectural remain is that of the mainly 14th century Chapel of St John of Jerusalem which has an earlier Norman door. The chapel has a recessed spire. It was heavily restored by Piers St Aubyn in 1886.

GARWAY

Henry II endowed the Templars with 2000 acres at Garway in the Monnow Valley in 1187 and they duly set up a commandery in this remote place. They were also given Lundy Island. In 1324 the property was transferred to the Hospitallers at Dinmore. The Commandery was on the site of Church House Farm. In 1512 the land was leased to Richard and Roger Mynors for 21 years. The only medieval survival of the Commandery is the memorable dovecote with 666 pigeon holes; it has an inscription which reads "1326 factum fuit istud columbarium per [fratrem] Ricardum". In 1397 the Bishop of Hereford complained the priest could not speak Welsh to his parishioners. In the early 16th century there were rows about the payment

Above, Dinmore, the Chapel of St John of Jerusalem.

Below, Garway, the Dovecote.

of ecclesiastical dues to the Bishop. Most of the villagers of Garway remained Catholic for 200 years after 1540, as evidenced by fines and confiscations. The earliest surviving part of the evocative church of St Michael is the sturdy detached fortified tower of 1180. The chancel is early 13th century and the nave late 13th century. The roof dates from c1400. The chancel arch is Norman with chevrons. There is a 14th century font. Old coffin lids have been used in the construction. There are carvings on the exterior wall of the church including a "Maltese" cross and an Agnus Dei. The foundations of the round nave of the earlier Templar church were excavated in 1927.

HAREWOOD

The park, part of the extensive royal forest, was given to the Templars of Garway by King John in 1215. They also received the advowson of the church of St Denis. The church was rebuilt in 1873-4. (Harewood is the site of a new classical house being constructed for HRH The Prince of Wales by the architect Craig Hamilton).

HEREFORD

The Hospitallers possessed a hospital and chapel of St John in Hereford. Richard I granted 36 acres to the Hospitallers of Dinmore to build a hospice for the sick and infirm. The hospital was bought after 1564 by the Coningsbys. In 1614 Sir Thomas Coningsby built almshouses for "worn out soldiers and superannuated faithful servants". The almshouses are now run by

Garway, the Church of St Michael. Clockwise from the top: the chancel, the fortified tower, the "Maltese" cross carving on the exterior, traces of the foundations of the round nave, and the Norman chancel arch.

the Venerable Order. The red sandstone Chapel has evidence of 13th century work, and the hall an early Perpendicular west window. The medieval stained glass considerably improved by Hardman comes from the former Hospitaller chapel at Harewood House.

St Giles's Hospital also belonged to the Hospitallers and the 18th century chapel has a reset Norman tympanum *(below)*.

Top: Hereford, the hospital and chapel of St John, with views of the interior and stained glass.

MARSTOW

The Hospitallers had the advowson of the church, of which there are no remains.

OXENHALL

60 acres and the advowson of the Church of St Anne was given to the Hospitallers of Dinmore. The tower of the church was built in the 14th century but the rest of the church was rebuilt in the 19th century.

SUTTON ST MICHAEL

The Hospitallers at Dinmore had a camera in this village which possessed some 350 acres of land. In the late 12th century the Priory of St Guthlac in Hereford made over the church of Sutton St Michael to the Hospitallers. It has a Norman nave and chancel, now rather fetchingly decorated in green. The font with four fine statues of lions at the base is also Norman.

WELSH NEWTON

The Templars of Garway possessed some 100 acres of land in Welsh Newton as well as the advowson of the Church of St Mary. These passed to the Hospitallers after 1312. The church is mostly 13th century. Its glory is the 13th century stone rood screen of c 1330 with its ball flower decoration. The wagon roof is c 1500. There are various medieval coffin slabs.

WORMBRIDGE

The Hospitallers of Dinmore were granted the manor and 200 acres of land by Richard I in 1189. They also had the advowson of the church of St Peter. There is a Norman north doorway of c1200. The nave and west tower are 13th

Clockwise from top left: Oxenhall, St Anne's Church; Sutton St Michael, the nave, exterior view and two details of the font.

century. Most of the rest of the church was heavily Victorianised. There are quite a lot of fragments of medieval glass - saints from the 14th century and a Virgin and Child of c1500.

OTHER

The Knights Hospitaller in 1540 had various other properties in Herefordshire including ones at Bodenham, Bridgnorth, Broomfield, Kentchurch, Lyonshall, Pedwardine, Rollestone (200 acres) and Wellington.

Right: Welsh Newton, the Church of St Mary.

Below: Wormbridge, the Church of St Peter. Below left, fragments of medieval glass and the nave.

HERTFORDSHIRE

BALDOCK

Gilbert de Clare, Earl of Pembroke gave 120 acres in Baldock to the Templars in 1152. They constructed the Church of St Mary the Virgin of which they also had the advowson. Both property and advowson passed to the Hospitallers after 1308. The advowson together with that of Weston was seized by Edward III in 1359 on no particularly justifiable grounds. The original church was built by the Templars in around 1150 and the east wall of the chancel survives from this date. The rest of the church was substantially rebuilt in the 1330s. The font is 13th century. Various slabs and brasses can be found.

ROYSTON

An underground bell-shaped cave may have links with the Templars. It has shallow religious carvings scratched in the chalk of St John the Baptist, a crowned lady, a Templar cross, St Lawrence and his grid iron, etc.

STANDON

Gilbert de Clare granted Rectory Manor (alias Standon Friars), 180 acres, a vineyard and the advowson of the church to the Hospitallers in the early 12th century. The manor appears to have been leased out from 1430 onwards. After the Dissolution the manor was acquired by Sir Ralph Sadleir. No traces of the manor remain but a building called Standon Hospice does survive. Sir Ralph Sadleir continued to feed the poor from here after the Dissolution. From 1612 to 1980 it functioned as a school. It is in the main of medieval construction. The chancel of the Church of St Mary dates from 1230-40. The chancel arch is lavishly

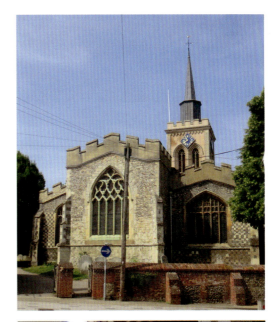

Right: Baldock, the Church of St Mary the Virgin, exterior and interior views, the 13th century font and one of the slabs.

Standon, the Church of St Mary: above, the memorial to Sir Ralph Sadleir, exterior, and right, the chancel arch and font.

carved. The nave is 14th century. The font is early 13th century (described in the *Shell Guide* as "so very Art Nouveauish"). There is a memorial with effigy to Sir Ralph Sadleir who died in 1587. He was an associate of Thomas Cromwell and fought against the Scots at the Battle of Pinkie.

TEMPLE DINSLEY

A Templar commandery was founded on land given by Bernard de Balliol in 1147. It was probably quite important as a number of chapters of the Templars were held here. Both Jacques de Molay, the last Grand Master, and Himbert Peaut, the last Visitor, stayed here, as did Henry III. It certainly possessed a chapel, hall, bakehouse and smithy. It also held some 400 acres of land. A broken stone effigy

from Temple Dinsley of an associate of the Templars (possibly Bernard de Balliol) can be found in St Mary's Church, Hitchin. Four Templars were arrested at Dinsley in 1308. After 1324 the Commandery was taken over by the Hospitallers and a camera was established here. After 1498 it appears to have been leased out. In 1543 Sir Ralph Sadleir built a mansion and park on the site. The Georgian Princess Helena College now stands on the site of the Commandery.

WESTON

The manor of Lannock was granted to the Templars by Gilbert de Clare, first Earl of Pembroke, who died in 1148. It passed to the Hospitallers, and after the Dissolution to Sir Michael Dormer. The site is now a farm. The Church of Holy Trinity was also granted to the Hospitallers in 1148 although the advowson was effectively seized in 1359 by Edward III on no very good grounds. Thereafter the Crown appointed. The cruciform church

Stone effigy originally from Temple Dinsley, now to be found at St Mary's Church Hitchin.

of the 12th century is still represented by nave, tower and north transept. The south aisle and roof are 15th century.

OTHER

The Knights Hospitaller in 1540 had various other properties in Hertfordshire including ones at Aldenham, Aspenden, Barkston, Bengeo, Broxbourne (150 acres and a mill), Buckland (formerly Templar), Buntingford, Charlton, (formerly Templar), and Hitchin (formerly Templar).

HUNTINGDONSHIRE

The Templars had lands at Folkesworth and Ogerston.

Weston, the Church of Holy Trinity, exterior and interior views.

KENT

BURHAM

In 1295 Boniface VIII appropriated the Church of the Blessed Virgin Mary to the Hospitallers, and the advowson remained with them until the Dissolution. The church was originally Norman, and then enlarged in the 14th century. It has two Norman fonts. The church is now in the care of the Churches Conservation Trust.

CAPEL

The Hospitallers had the advowson of the Church of St Thomas à Becket the Martyr which was given to the Commandery of West Peckham. The tower and nave date from around 1400. The wall paintings on the north side of the nave are 13th century. The church is now in the care of the Churches Conservation Trust.

DOVER

Bredenstone Hill on the south west side of the town belonged to the Templars, and subsequently the Hospitallers. The foundations of a small medieval church with a circular nave which belonged to the Templars was discovered in 1806.

Above: Burham, the Church of the Blessed Virgin Mary.
Below and left: wall paintings from the Church of St Thomas à Becket the Martyr, Capel.

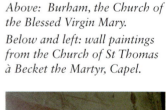

Above: exterior and interior views of the Church of St Thomas à Becket the Martyr, Capel.

Left: Dover, Bredenstone Hill.

Below: Hadlow, the Church of St Mary, exterior and interior showing the chancel arch.

HADLOW

The advowson of the Church of St Mary was given to the Commandery of West Peckham in 1216. The tower/spire and chancel arch are 13th century. The chancel was rebuilt by the Hospitallers shortly after they acquired it. Much of the rest of the church has been heavily Victorianised.

RODMERSHAM

The Church of St Nicholas was given by Henry II to the Hospital of St John of Jerusalem, a donation confirmed by King John in 1199. It subsequently became attached to the Commandery based at West Peckham in Kent. In 1540 the living went to the Crown but in 1545 it was given to John Porage, who lived in the village of Rodmersham. The church is Perpendicular with a dark flint tower. It has been heavily restored. Three wooden seats in the chancel with wooden canopies are medieval.

Above: Rodmersham, the Church of St Nicholas, exterior and interior showing the three medieval seats in the chancel.

SHIPBOURNE

The Church of St Giles was appropriated to the Hospitallers. There are apparently fragmentary 14th century remains (invisible to the author's eye) predating the rebuilding of the church by James Gibbs in 1721-2. This church was in its turn demolished and replaced by a new church built for Edward Cazalet in 1879-81.

STROOD

The manor was given in 1159 to the Templars by Henry II. After their suppression the manor should in 1312 have gone to the Hospitallers. Edward II however continued to hold the lands and in 1342 the manor was ceded to the Crown. In 1342 Edward III granted the manor to Mary de St Pol, Countess of Pembroke who in turn granted it to her Franciscan nunnery at Denny in Cambridgeshire (qv). Temple Manor is now situated in the middle of an industrial estate. It suffered bomb damage during the Second World War. It is owned, after restoration, by English Heritage. The 13th century flint manor house dating from c1240 is complete, a first floor room on a vaulted undercroft.

Strood: exterior view and the first floor room.

April to October). The 13th century Hospitaller chapel dedicated to St John the Baptist with its lancet windows survives, although earlier tenants inserted a floor half way up in order to make a billiard room.

SWINGFIELD

Swingfield ("the field of swine") was occupied by some sisters of St John until they were removed to Buckland in Somerset c.1180. The Hospitallers then seemed to have taken possession and set up a commandery. Total receipts in 1338 were £82 4s 4d. That year the inhabitants included the Commander Ralph Basset, a brother, three chaplains, two clerks, nine servants and the holder of a corrody. A later Commander, Daniel de Carreto, was recommended by Urban V to be Prior in Rome. In the 1520s

SUTTON-AT-HONE

Robert de Basing gave the manor of Sutton to the Knights Hospitaller in 1199. A commandery was established. Henry III was a regular visitor, staying 15 times between 1232 and 1264. The Commandery held about 60 acres from the King on the condition that it distributed peas and bread to the poor three times a week. By 1338 the property was leased out. The manor was granted to Sir Maurice Denys in 1540. The site of the 16th century manor (St John's Jerusalem) located on a moated site fed by the River Darent is now owned by the National Trust (open Wednesdays

Above: Strood, the vaulted undercroft.
Below: the Manor at Sutton-at-Hone and its chapel.

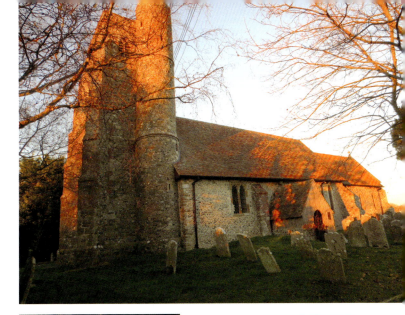

the Prior of Ireland, Sir John Rawson, used the Commandery as his English residence. In 1540 it passed to Sir Anthony Aucher of Orterden who subsequently sold it to Sir Henry Palmer of Wingham. A complete knapped flint chapel of c1230 with lancets and two storeyed hall survive, now in the care of English Heritage. The advowson of the Church of St Peter was also given to the Hospitallers and is now in the care of the Churches Conservation Trust. The church is flint and has a tall Perpendicular western tower. The roof is 14th century. It was fairly heavily restored by the Victorians.

TEMPLE EWELL

A Templar commandery was set up at Temple Ewell before 1163. It was given to them by William, the brother of Henry II and William de Peverell, Constable of Dover Castle. The estate was 300 acres by 1185. According to the chronicler Matthew Paris, King John made his submission to Pandulph, the papal legate, on 15th May 1213 "in the house of the Templars near Dover", which must have been Temple Ewell. The Hospitallers obtained possession after 1312. The Commandery passed through a number of hands after 1540, starting with Lord Clinton and Saye.

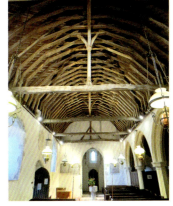

Above: Swingfield, the hall, chapel and Church of St Peter.

Right: Temple Ewell, the Church of St Peter and St Paul.

No traces remain. The advowson of the Church of St Peter and St Paul was given to the Templars and passed to the Hospitallers. The church is of flint with nave and chancel in one. There is a Norman north doorway and a 13th century chancel arch.

TILMANSTONE

The advowson of the Church of St Andrew was given to the Hospitallers at Swingfield by Archbishop Stephen Langton during the reign of King John although he retained the right to appoint the vicar who retained a moiety of the tithes. The nave and north chancel of the flint building retain their Norman windows. The west tower is 14th century and the chancel arch also 14th. The font is Norman.

Below: Tilmanstone, the Church of St Andrew.

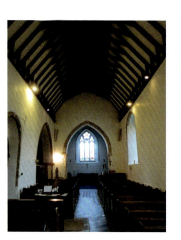

TONBRIDGE

Roger de Clare, Earl of Hertford, gave the advowson of the Church of St Peter and St Paul to the Hospitallers of West Peckham. The earliest part of the church is the chancel with a Norman north window. The north arcade is 13th century while the battlemented west tower and the chancel arch are 14th century. The building was heavily restored by Ewan Christian in 1877-9.

Below: interior and exterior views of the Church of St Peter and St Paul, Tonbridge.

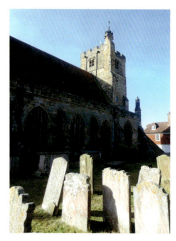

WEST PECKHAM

Sir John Colepepper, one of the judges of common pleas, gave lands to the Hospitallers in 1408 and a commandery was established. It was known as the Chantry Magistrale as its revenues went directly to the Grand Master. After the Dissolution the property went to Sir Richard Southwell of Mereworth. Duke's Place may have been the residence of the receiver of the estate. This large, half timbered L shaped house dates back to the 15th century.

OTHER

The Knights Hospitaller in 1540 had various other properties in Kent including those at Ash, Bilchester, Bonnington, Brookland, Canterbury, Eythorne, Hawley, Hoo, Liddon (Cockescombe Manor and 420 acres), Mereworth, Ore, Patrixbourne, Radfield and Stallisfield.

Right: West Peckham, Duke's Place.

LANCASHIRE

STYDD (RIBCHESTER)

The Hospitallers arrived in Stydd by 1150 and set up a hospice and a chapel. Their church of St Saviour survives although the domestic buildings have disappeared. It is built in of sandstone rubble and has a nave and chancel in one. There are two Norman windows in the north wall, and Perpendicular windows on the south side. The font is late Perpendicular. There is a foliated stone slab which marks the grave of Sir Adam de Cliderow and his wife Lady Alicia. One of the gravestones with an engraved cross is said to be that of St Margaret Clitherow. There is also an 18th century stone slab to Francis Petre, Vicar Apostolic of the Northern District and Titular Bishop of Armorium who died in 1775. There is a holy well in the graveyard.

The Knights Hospitaller in 1540 had various other properties in Lancashire including ones at Crompton (or Cropton) (140 acres), Cuerden, Howarth (40 acres) and Leyland (135 acres).

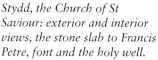

Stydd, the Church of St Saviour: exterior and interior views, the stone slab to Francis Petre, font and the holy well.

LEICESTERSHIRE

ASHBY PARVA

The advowson of the Church of St Peter was granted to the Commandery of Dalby. The church has a low rebuilt 14th century tower and a Perpendicular nave. The font is Norman.

BUCKMINSTER

The advowson of the Church of St John Baptist was granted to the Commandery of Dalby in 1237; in 1388 the advowson was transferred to the Prior and Convent of Kirkby Bellars. The church is constructed

Above: Ashby Parva, the Church of St Peter.

Left and below: the Church of St John Baptist, Buckminster.

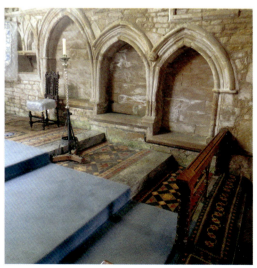

in grey oolite. The tower, chancel sedilia, double piscina and Easter Sepulchre all date to the second half of the 13th century. The arcades and north aisle windows are 14th century. The chancel and font are Perpendicular. The roof is supported by angels.

DALBY AND HEATHER

Lands at Dalby consisting of some 1,440 acres were originally said to have been given to the Hospitallers by Robert Le Bossu, Earl of Leicester. A commandery seems to have been established there by 1206. By 1371 the Commandery had been united with that of Rothley. No traces remain. The advowson of the Church of St Swithin was granted to the Hospitallers. The tower and chancel are medieval but the nave was destroyed when the spire collapsed in 1658 and rebuilt in a vaguely medieval style. Some modern glass records the link of the church with the Knights Hospitaller.

ROTHLEY TEMPLE

The Templars possessed land at Rothley by 1203, and a commandery was established in 1231 when Henry III granted the Manor. The estate was transferred to the Hospitallers after 1308 and united with Dalby in 1371. The late 13th century chapel survives as part of

Top, left and right: Dalby and Heather, Church of St Swithin.

Above: the chapel at Rothley Court Hotel, exterior and interior views.

Left: the alabaster slab in the Church of St John the Baptist, Rothley Temple.

the Rothley Court Hotel. There are lancet windows although the east window is Perpendicular. There is a defaced effigy under an ogee canopy. The advowson of the Church of St Mary and St John Baptist was also granted to the Templars and subsequently the Hospitallers. The church is large and constructed of pink granite. It is basically Perpendicular although the arcades are late 13th century. The font is Norman. A pre-Reformation alabaster slab survives.

Above and right, the Church of St John the Baptist, Rothley Temple.

SWINFORD

In around 1190 Robert Revel granted some 160 acres to the Hospitallers. A commandery was set up but seems to have come under the control of Dalby by 1220. In 1338 it is recorded as a camera. There are no remains of the domestic buildings. The advowson of the Church of All Saints was granted to the Commandery of Dalby. The north arcade is 13th century and the rest mainly 14th century. The chancel was rebuilt in the 18th century. The font is Norman.

Below and right, Swinford, the Church of All Saints.

The Knights Hospitaller in 1540 had various other properties in Leicestershire including one at Baggrave (450 acres).

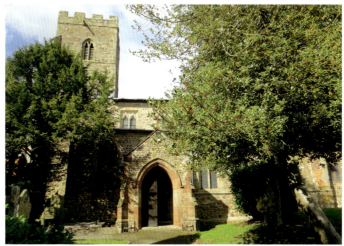

GAZETTEER: LEICESTERSHIRE

LINCOLNSHIRE

ALTHORPE

The Templars were given some 160 acres of land by Roger de Mowbray. The advowson of the Church of St Oswald was similarly granted. The Hospitallers obtained both land and advowson after 1312. In 1519 the rector Radalfus Babington was non-resident and the rectory leased. The church is mainly 15th century and has the arms of the Nevilles (a Lincolnshire family which provided a number of Hospitallers in the late 15th/early 16th centuries) on the tower.

ASHBY-DE-LA-LAUNDE

In 1185 the Templars held 38 bovates (c 570 acres) in the village. The advowson of the Church of St Hibald was granted to the Templars of Temple Bruer. The Hospitallers successfully gained possession of both land and advowson after 1312. The west tower and spire of the church are 13th/14th century but the rest of the church was rebuilt in 1854.

ASLACKBY

1200 acres of land at Aslackby (which the Reverend Henry Thorold, in the *Shell Guide* of Lincolnshire, assures us is pronounced "Ayzlelby") was given to the Templars by Hubert of Rye in the 1160s. Other gifts followed and a commandery was set up. After 1312 the Hospitallers gained possession but

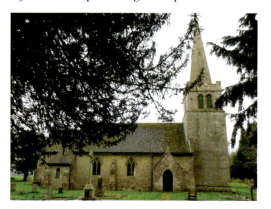

Above: Althorpe, the Church of St Oswald: exterior and interior views, and the arms of the Neville family.

Left: Ashby-de-la-Launde, the Church of St Hibald.

  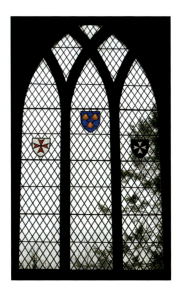

never had a commandery here, the land passing to Temple Bruer. Temple Farm is east of the church. The gatehouse and a vaulted undercroft remained until 1887. A head of a two-light 15th century window can still be found. The Templars, then Hospitallers, also had the advowson of the Church of St James. The church has a very grand Perpendicular square tower and a spacious clerestoried interior. The chancel is of 1856. The Hospitallers are recorded in some modern stained glass.

Aslackby, St James' Church, the tower, interior and modern glass. Below: Boston, St Botolph's.

BOSTON

The Hospitallers were granted the now vanished Hospital of St Leonard in 1230 by Sir Thomas Moulton, and it changed its name to the Hospital of St John. The advowson of the Church of St Botolph lay with the Abbey and Convent of St Mary's York until 1486 when it was swapped with the Crown. The Crown then in turn swapped it with the Hospitallers for certain lands in Leicestershire. The

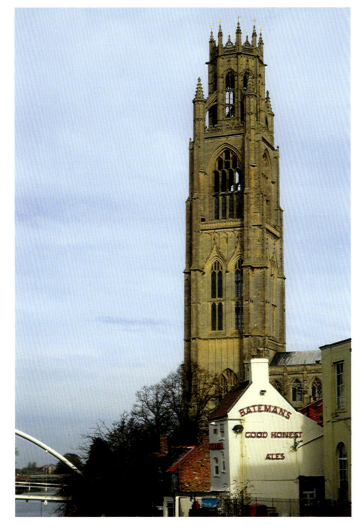

latter retained the advowson until the Dissolution. The large church was rebuilt in the 14th century. It is however best known for its 272 foot high Perpendicular tower known as the "Stump". ("Some stump!" – Henry Thorold.) The effigy of a knight on a tomb in the church has often been stated to be wearing the cross of the order but it is not strictly that; it may be the cross of a donat, a giver to the order. Several Knights of Rhodes were members of the Guild of Corpus Christi in the 15th century.

This page: St Botolph's Church, Boston, interior and exterior views. Above: the effigy of a knight, possibly a donat.

BOTTESFORD

The Hospitallers had a camera of 150 acres, a dovecote and a water mill at Bottesford (now effectively a suburb of Scunthorpe) given to them by Simon de Vere, nephew of the Prior, in 1207. There are no remains. They also possessed the advowson of the Church of St Peter in Chains. "This is one of the finest pure Early English churches anywhere, and deserves to be better known. The nave is lofty and clerestoried, and the chancel is as lofty as

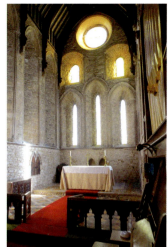

the nave. There are grand narrow transepts - and everywhere long narrow lancet windows, especially and strikingly so in the chancel...It is all the work of the greatest refinement." (The Reverend Henry Thorold "Lincolnshire Churches Revisited").

CAYTHORPE

The Templars, then the Hospitallers held c 75 acres of land. They were also given the advowson of the Church of St Vincent. The church is 14th century with twin naves divided by arcades and a spire with flying buttresses.

DONINGTON

The advowson of the Church of St Mary and the Holy Rood was given to the Templars c 1285 and subsequently taken over by the Hospitallers. The church seem to have been appropriated to the priory of nuns at Buckland. The building is a mixture of Decorated and Perpendicular with a

Above: Bottesford, St Peter in Chains.

Below, Caythorpe, the Church of St Vincent.

grand south west tower and spire crowning a spacious vaulted porch. The interior has grand arcades with carved corbles and a Perpendicular font.

Above and right: Donnington, the Church of St Mary, with its Perpendicular font and carved corbles.

EAGLE

Eagle was a major Templar commandery on lands of some 900 acres said to have been given by King Stephen. It was used as an infirmary. 8 Templars were arrested there in 1308. It was transferred to the Hospitallers after 1312. It became the Capitular Bailiwick of the Langue of England in 1433. It was one of the richest commanderies. No traces of the Commandery however remain. The Hospitallers also had the advowson of the Church of All Saints. The low unbuttressed west tower is Early English and the font Norman. The rest of the church is Edwardian. William Langstrother, Bailiff of Eagle in the mid 15th century, presented the church with relics of St Zita from Lucca. In the east wall there is an inscription "To the glory of God, this stone was laid on the rebuilding of the church, the ancient possession of the Order of St John of Jerusalem, July 14th, 1903." The Victorian lychgate records the historic involvement of the Order.

Above: Eagle, the Church of All Saints

GAINSBOROUGH

The advowson of the Church of All Saints was given to the Templar Commandery of Willoughton. The 90 foot Perpendicular west tower survives but the rest of the church was rebuilt in the 18th century. *(Below)*

Above and right: Goulceby, the Church of All Saints,

GOULCEBY

The advowson of the Church of All Saints was given to the Templar Commandery of Willoughton. The church is mainly of 1908 but old materials were used. There is a Perpendicular font.

GREAT LIMBER

Great Limber (or Limber Magna) was a camera of the Templars with 300 acres, subsequently transferred to the Hospitallers. Some earthworks survive. The estate was eventually bought by the Pelhams. (Limber is chiefly known as the site of James Wyatt's Brocklesby Mausoleum of 1787-94).

HAREBY

The advowson of the Church of St Peter and St Paul was given to the Templar Commandery of Willoughton. The church is largely of 1858 but incorporates earlier fragments including the charming little Decorated niche above the west door.

HORKSTOW

Horkstow was a Templar camera, subsequently transferred to the Hospitallers. There are no remains. The Templars also had the advowson of the Church of St Maurice. The church has Early English arcades, chancel arch and chancel. (The artist George Stubbs lived in the village for a number of years in the 18th century).

LINCOLN

There appears to have been a small Hospitaller commandery in 1257. It had however ceased to exist by 1338. No traces remain.

Right: Hareby, the Church of St Peter and St Paul, with the decorated niche above the west door.

Below: Horkstow, the Church of St Maurice.

tomb. The advowson of the now vanished Church of St John Baptist, Little Carbrooke, was also made over to the Hospitallers but this church closed in 1424 for lack of parishioners and has vanished.

HADDISCOE

There was a Templar commandery here on land given by Henry III but it was dissolved after 1308. No traces remain.

The Knights Hospitaller in 1540 had various other lands in Norfolk including ones at Bawburgh (64 acres), Costessy (110 acres) and Togrynd (formerly Templar, 50 acres)

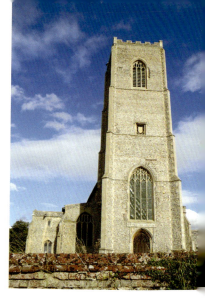

This page: the Church of St Peter and St Paul, Great Carbrooke, and below the earthworks south-east of the church.

NORTHAMPTONSHIRE

BLAKESLEY

The manor was granted to the Hospitallers in the 13th century. Priory Farm has a medieval roof and Blakesley House is supposed to have some remains. The advowson of the Church of St Mary was given to the Hospitaller Commandery of Melchbourne. The ironstone church is mainly heavily restored Decorated. The south chapel is Perpendicular. The roof is supported on corbels of music making angels. There is a brass to Matthew Swetenham, bow-bearer to Henry IV, who died in 1416.

Above and right: Blakesley, the Church of St Mary and the brass to Matthew Swetenham.

DINGLEY

A Hospitaller commandery existed here on the site of what is now the late 16th century Dingley Hall. It was founded in the reign of King Stephen and had 300 acres of land. In 1338 a handsome balance of £42 3s 8d was paid to the general treasury of the Grand Prior. After 1454 Dingley was combined with the Commandery of Battisford in Sussex. Sir Giles Russell, Lieutenant Turcopolier, was the last Commander of Dingley. The advowson of the Church of All Saints only came to the Hospitallers as late as 1448. The church is 12th century in origin although the windows and the tower are Perpendicular. (Admiral Lord Beatty obit 1936 lies in the graveyard.)

Below: Dingley, the Church of All Saints.

Bottom: Guilsborough, the Church of St Etheldreda.

GUILSBOROUGH

A Hospitaller camera existed here in 1338; no traces remain. The advowson of the Church of St Etheldreda was appropriated to the Hospitaller Commandery of Dingley. The church is mainly 14th century.

HARGRAVE

The advowson of the Church of All Hallows seems to have been claimed by the Hospitallers at one stage but in 1228

was finally lost to Richard de Deseburg. The church is early 13th century in origin but was heavily restored by the Victorians.

RAVENSTHORPE

The advowson of the Church of St Denis belonged to the Hospitallers. The arcades and the tower are of the 13th century.

The Knights Hospitaller in 1540 had various other properties in Northamptonshire including 530 acres at Harrington.

Top: Guilsborough, the Church of St Etheldreda, porch, chancel arch and roof.
Above: Hargrave, the Church of All Hallows.
Below: Ravensthorpe, the Church of St Denis.

NORTHUMBERLAND

CHIBBURN

The Commandery of the Hospitallers at Chibburn is first mentioned in 1313 and was situated on the pilgrimage route to Lindisfarne. The buildings consisted of a domestic residence, chapel etc enclosing a central courtyard. In 1540 the land and buildings went to the Crown and then to the Widdringtons. The Commandery is now ruinous and surrounded by the remains of open cast coal mining. Encircled by the remains of a moat, the east and west walls, and part of the north wall of the 14th century chapel still stand.

TEMPLE THORNTON

A Templar commandery was founded before 1205 on land given to them by William de Lisle. Four Templars were arrested there in 1308. The site subsequently became a Hospitaller camera. No traces remain. The nearby Church of St Andrew, Hartburn, was used by the Templars after 1250 although seemingly not appropriated. A "Maltese" cross has been carved on the right side of the southern door.

Above: the ruins at Chibburn.

Right: Hartburn, the Church of St Andrew with the "Maltese" cross carving.

Below: Averham, the Church of St Michael.

NOTTINGHAMSHIRE

AVERHAM (CHURCH)

The beautifully situated Church of St Michael was granted to the Commandery of Ossington before 1199 by Henry Hosatus. There is much Norman herringbone masonry in the tower and body of the church. The Perpendicular porch and tower are adorned by the arms of the Suttons. There is an impressive interior with a spacious aisleless nave and chancel. The chancel roof is gaily painted. A considerable amount of medieval glass survives.

Left and above: Averham, St Michael's, tomb, interior and medieval glass.

Below: St Wilfrid's, Low Marnham, interior and exterior views, the porch door and glass.

however 13th century. The south was probably built by masons from Lincoln with tall octagonal pillars and detached shafts. The north side has low cylindrical piers of local design. The south door has an elaborate ogee arch. There is 15th century stained glass of St James. The church now belongs to the Churches Conservation Trust.

LOW MARNHAM

The Church of St Wilfrid was granted to the Hospitaller Commandery of Ossington by 1230 when the grant was confirmed by Walter de Gray, Archbishop of York. The church is externally 15th century Perpendicular. The arcades and chancel arch inside are

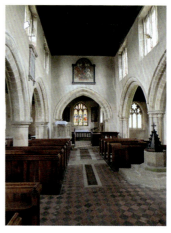

MAPLEBECK

The Church of St Radegund (St John until 1895) was originally a chapel attached to the Hospitaller camera at Winkburn. The church is heavily restored. The tower and broach spire are 14th century. The north arcade is a little earlier; stone medieval altar rails have been attached to the wall. One lancet window remains at the east end of the chancel.

OSSINGTON

The Commandery was founded in the mid 12th century. Ossington Church was granted to the Commandery by "Archbishop William" (presumably St William Fitzherbert, Archbishop of York 1143-54). Henry III granted free warren over the demesne lands. In the late 12th century the village of Ossington was granted by Roger de Buron. He however in later life joined the Cluniac Priory of Lenton to whom he also granted the village. Considerable litigation ensued. However in 1204 Roger's son Walter Smallet confirmed the grant to the Commandery; Lenton did not drop its claim until 1208.

The Commandery possessed some 600 acres of land and in 1338 the revenue of the Commandery was £85 8s 8d and the expenditure £77 7s. The Commandery held lands in Danethorpe (82 acres), Kneesall and Winkburn as well as Ossington. In 1382 Ossington was made part of the Commandery of Newland in Yorkshire. In the Valor Ecclesiasticus of 1534 the yield of "Ossington Bailiwick" was reckoned at £20. Nothing survives of the Commandery; the 1782 charming classical Church of the Holy Rood by Carr of York is believed to have been built on the site. It contains the tomb and brass of Reynald Peckham (obit 1551), married to a Cartwright, which family obtained the property at the Dissolution.

Above: Maplebeck, the Church of St Radegund, exterior and interior views, showing the medieval altar rails.

Below: Sibthorpe, the Church of St Peter, the Easter Sepulchre and Dovecote.

SIBTHORPE

The Church of St Peter was granted to the Templar Commandery of Eagle in Lincolnshire before 1230 when the grant was confirmed by Walter de Gray, Archbishop of York. The tower and the chancel arch date from the 13th century. In 1324 Thomas de Sibthorpe rebuilt the rest of the church and set up a college of priests which was surrendered to Henry VIII in 1540. In 1341 he managed to obtain the advowson from the Hospitallers.

A small beautiful 14th century Easter Sepulchre with its original colour survives on the north wall of the chancel. In the field nearby stands a great 14th century dovecote, round and tall, with a conical roof.

WINKBURN

At some stage before 1199 the Church of St John of Jerusalem at Winkburn was granted to the Commandery of Ossington by Henry Hosatus. The manor with 600 acres was granted subsequently by one Adam Tyson. A camera was duly set up, and in 1534 this had an income of £19. The camera buildings have vanished. The manor was granted to William Burnell in 1548. The Hall is 18th century and is owned by the Craven-Smith-Milnes. The Church of St John of Jerusalem stands next to the Hall. The Norman tower was rebuilt in 1623 using Norman materials. The south door is Norman and there is one lancet window. The chief charm of the church is, however, the unspoilt Georgian interior.

The Knights Hospitallers in 1540 had a number of other mainly small properties in Nottinghamshire.

Below: Winkburn, the Church of St John of Jerusalem.
Right: Broadwell, the Church of St Peter and St Paul, with the font and south door below.

OXFORDSHIRE

BROADWELL

The manor of Bradwell St John was a Templar possession of some 600 acres belonging to Temple Guiting and given by Alan de Limesy. It was seized by Edward II in 1308 and given to Hugh le Despenser. In 1340 it belonged to Sir William de Clinton, Earl of Huntingdon. However it was subsequently regained by the Hospitallers and came under their Commandery of Quenington in Gloucestershire. No traces of the manor remain. The advowson of the Church of St Peter and St Paul was given to the Templars and was firmly in Hospitaller hands by 1348. ("A church to see" John Piper – *Shell Guide*). The church is large, late Norman with 13th century additions. The west tower has a 13th century octagonal spire. The south door and font are Norman.

CLANFIELD

A Hospitaller commandery was set up in 1279. It possessed some 670 acres of land. By 1433 it had merged with Quenington. The site of the Commandery was at Friar's Court, one mile south of the village. The moated site, but none of the medieval buildings, remains.

GOSFORD

The manor of Gosford (now a suburb of Kidlington) was given to the Hospitallers in 1142. By 1433 it came under the Commandery of Quenington. No traces remain.

HARDWICK

The advowson of the Church of St Mary was in the hands of the Hospitallers by 1252. The Prior of St John appointed until 1540 with one exception in 1482 when the bishop collated by lapse. The nave is 15th century and the chancel 14th century. There is a modern statue of Our Lady over the porch. Two panels of medieval glass of Christ in Majesty and the Crucifixion remain in the west window.

KELMSCOTT

The Church of St George was originally a chapel which came under the church of Broadwell (a Templar advowson), which appointed the vicars. The church is small and rural. The nave and chancel are

Transitional Norman of c1190. The transepts and bellcote are 13th century as is the font. There are some 14th century wall paintings and medieval stained glass of St George.

KIDLINGTON

The St John Ambulance building has inside an oak 15th century four light window which is supposed to have come from the Hospitaller Louse Hall.

MERTON

The manor of Merton was granted to the Templars by Simon de Senlis, Earl of Huntingdon, in 1152-3. In 1313 it was assigned to the Hospitallers of Sandford on Thames. The estate consisted of some 300 acres. No traces remain.

Above: all that remains of the Commandery at Clanfield.

Below: the Church of St Mary at Hardwick with its 14th century glass, and below an exterior view.

SANDFORD-ON-THAMES

In about 1240, Thomas, son of Thomas de Sandford, gave his lands at Sandford to the Templars. He himself became a Templar at Temple Cowley although shortly afterwards the headquarters of the Commandery moved to Sandford. In 1312 the lands (250 acres plus two watermills) were transferred to the Hospitallers. The former Commandery was taken over as early as 1524 by Cardinal Wolsey and passed to the King in 1530. Temple Farm is the site of the Commandery. It is mainly an 18th century building (now a hotel) but has some 15th century remains such as a cross pattee, a four light window which may be from the chapel etc. The advowson of the Church of St Andrew lay originally with the nuns of Littlemore Priory of which the Templars were patrons. From 1338 onwards the Hospitallers seemed to have presented. The church was rebuilt by James Brooks in 1865 although one or two earlier features survive. There is a 15th century alabaster carving of the Assumption of Our Lady with some gilding which acted as a step in the churchyard until rediscovered in the 19th century and moved into the church. It may have come from the chapel of the Commandery.

Above: Kelmscott, St George's Church, exterior, interior, wall painting and glass.

Below: Kidlington: the window preserved in the St John Ambulance building.

Bottom: Sandford, the cross pattee.

THE KNIGHTS HOSPITALLER IN GREAT BRITAIN IN 1540

TEMPLE COWLEY

In 1139 Maud, Countess of Boulogne, Stephen's Queen, gave all her land in Cowley to the Templars. Further land was given in 1220 by John Marshal of Ireland, a kinsman of the Earl of Pembroke. After the suppression of the Templars all the land was held temporarily by Queen Margaret but it soon went to the Hospitallers. The estate consisted of over 340 acres of land. The lands were leased in the early 16th century. No traces remain.

WESTCOTT

The Hospitallers had land in the parish in 1279. No traces remain.

WESTWELL

The advowson of St Mary's Church was given to the Hospitallers of Quenington by the de Hastings family. The advowson may have later passed to Edington Priory. The church is basically 12th century with a Norman south doorway. The font is of c 1200. There is fragmentary medieval glass.

The Knights Hospitaller in 1540 had various other properties in Oxfordshire including ones at Calverton (formerly Templar), Garsington, Horspath (formerly Templar, 880 acres), Littlemore (120 acres), Merton (formerly Templar), Oxford and Sibford Ferris/Sibford Gower (200 acres).

Below and right: Westwell, St Mary's Church.

Above: Sandford-on-Thames: Temple Farm, the alabaster carving of the Assumption of Our Lady and exterior of the Church of St Andrew.

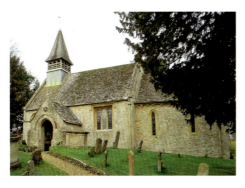  

PEMBROKESHIRE

AMBLESTON

The advowson of the church of St Mary was given to the Hospitallers of Slebech by Wizo the Fleming between 1162 and 1176. The chancel and nave are 13th-14th century. The tower was rebuilt in the 18th century. The font is 12th-13th century.

AMROTH

290 acres and the advowson of the Church of St Elidyr was given to the Hospitallers of Slebech in 1150. The church was rebuilt in the 13th century, and added to in the 15th. There is a good Norman font with vine leaf foliage.

CASTELLAN

The chapel in the parish of Penrydd was granted to the Hospitallers by William Marshall, Earl of Pembroke c1130. It was ruinous by 1684 and has now vanished from the maps.

CLARBESTON

The advowson of the Church of St Martin was given to the Hospitallers of Slebech between 1162 and 1184. The church was rebuilt in 1841.

LETTERSTON WITH LLANFAIR NANT Y GOF (TRECWYN)

The advowson of the Church of St Giles was given to the Hospitallers by Ivo, son of Letard before 1130. The church was rebuilt by the Victorians but retains some earlier monuments and a scalloped Norman font. The advowson covered the chapel of St Mary of Llanfair Nant y Gof as well, which is also known as Trecwyn (completely rebuilt in 1855).

Top: St Mary's, Ambleston.

Above: the Church of St Elidyr, Amroth, and right, its Norman font.

LLANFYRNACH

100 acres and the advowson of the Church of St Brynach were granted to the Hospitallers of Slebech before 1165. The church was completely rebuilt in 1842.

MARTLETWY

240 acres and the advowson of the Church of St Marcellus was given to the Hospitallers of Slebech around 1150. The church was rebuilt in 1848-50 but retained a Norman font. In 2011 it was scheduled to be partially demolished and maintained as a ruin.

MINWEAR

Robert, son of Lomer, granted a manor of some 540 acres and the advowson of the Church of St Womar c 1150 to the Hospitallers of Slebech. The setting is adjacent to a farm, and idyllic. The church is basically 12th century. The interior is striking. There is a good medieval font.

PRENDERGAST

The advowson of the Church of St David was granted to the Hospitallers between 1162 and 1176. Prendergast is now a suburb of Haverfordwest. The church was built in 1191 but only the top of the tower and the porch are original. A metalwork gate may pay tribute to the Hospitallers.

ROSEMARKET

The advowson of the Church of St Ismael was

Top four: St Womar's, Minwear, interior and exterior views.

Above right and below: St David's, Prendergast, with its metalwork gate.

Right: St Ismael's, Rosemarket.

granted to the Hospitallers of Slebech in the 12th century. The church is 12th century in origin but heavily restored by the Victorians. The font is Norman.

ROCH

The advowson of the Church of St David was given to the Hospitallers of Slebech in the 12th century. The church was heavily restored by the Victorians. There is a 13th century font.

RUDBAXTON

The advowson of the Church of St Michael (previously St Madoc) was granted to the Hospitallers of Slebech between 1162 and 1176. The church is 14th-15th century.

SLEBECH

The estate of some 100 acres with a mill and fishpond was given to the Hospitallers by 1161 by Wizo, Lord of Wiston and endowed by the Clare Earls of Pembroke. The Commandery, situated on the pilgrimage route to St

Top: the Church of St David, Roch: exterior and the font.

Above: the Church of St Michael, Rudbaxton, exterior and interior views.

David's (in 1123 Pope Calixtus III declared two pilgrimages to St David's equalled one to Rome and three pilgrimages to St David's equalled one to Jerusalem) became the headquarters of the Hospitallers in West Wales. It was the richest Commandery outside Clerkenwell, with estates along the Welsh coast from north west to south east. Slebech at one time had no less than 31 churches attached to it. In 1338 it had an income of £307. At this time the occupants included the Commander John de Frouwyck, two brothers, a chaplain, four corrodary holders and thirteen servants. The 18th century Slebech Hall (recently sold) was the site of the Commandery. Slebech Old Church (St John the Baptist) was deliberately unroofed in 1844 by the Baron de Rutzen when the now abandoned new church was constructed. The Decorated nave, 15th century chancel, transepts and Perpendicular tower survive from the earlier church. A Hospitaller cross can be made out above the entrance. The font remains. The site on the Claddau estuary

Slebech: clockwise from the top, the site on the Claddau Estuary, the Decorated nave, transepts, font, Perpendicular tower and entrance with traces of a Hospitaller cross.

GAZETTEER: PEMBROKESHIRE

Wiston, the Church of St Mary.

is an evocative one. A fishpond also survives. The 15th century effigies of Sir Henry Wogan (obit 1475) and his wife in the church have been moved elsewhere.

UZMASTON

The advowson of the Church of St Ismael was granted to the Hospitallers of Slebech, probably before 1169. The church was virtually rebuilt 1872-03.

WALTON EAST

The advowson of the Church of St Mary Magdalen was given to the Hospitallers of Slebech. The church was rebuilt in 1839 to 1853. The font however is a 12th century scalloped bowl.

WISTON

The advowson of the church of St Mary was given to the Hospitallers of Slebech by Wizo the Fleming. The church is 13th century with 15th century accretions.

(The Hospitallers of Slebech also owned the advowsons of the churches of Lanelau, Rowistich and Stremenrick; the author has not been able to identify these places.)

The Knights Hospitaller in 1540 had various other properties in Pembrokeshire including ones at Blaiden (105 acres), Bochinfield (600 acres), Cuffern (240 acres), Dolbyyrvawr (120 acres), Stacpole (120 acres), Stokesbury (60 acres), Welsh Hook (240 acres).

RADNORSHIRE

LLANFIHANGEL NANT MELAN

The advowson of the Church of St Michael was given to the Hospitallers of Slebech between 1175 and 1198 by William de Braose. The church was rebuilt in 1846.

RUTLAND

STRETTON

The advowson of the Church of St Nicholas was granted to the Templars of South Witham by 1185. The advowson however did not go to the Hospitallers after the Dissolution of the Templars. The church has a simple Norman south doorway, a good 13th century north arcade and a 13th century chancel. The font is Early English.

The Church of St Nicholas, Stretton. Left: the Norman south doorway, and right, the exterior and the north arcade.

SHROPSHIRE

CARDINGTON

The advowson of the Church of St James was granted to the Templars by Bishop Vere in the late 12th century. The Hospitallers of Dinmore retained the advowson after 1312 although losing their lands in the parish to the Earl of Arundel. The church has a Norman nave. The west tower is Early English and the chancel was rebuilt in the late 13th century.

Above: St James' Church, Cardington: the west tower and interior.

Below: Clee St Margaret, the Church of St Margaret.

CLEE ST MARGARET

The advowson of the Church of St Margaret was granted to the Hospitallers of Dinmore. The church has a Norman chancel with herring bone work outside. There is a 13th century door and a Norman font.

ELLESMERE

The advowson of the Church of St Mary was acquired by the Hospitallers of Halston from Llewellyn the Great in

Left: Clee St Margaret, the Church of St Margaret, the Norman chancel.

Right: Ellesmere, St Mary's Church, exterior and below, the chancel chapel.

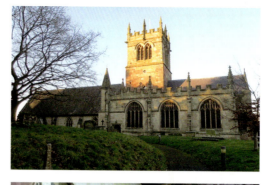

1225. The large cruciform church was substantially rebuilt by George Gilbert Scott in 1848-9. The Early English crossing was allowed to survive as was the early 14th century south chancel chapel.

HALSTON

The Commandery was founded between 1165 and 1187 when Roger de Powys, Lord of Whittington, gave a portion of his demesne to the Hospitallers. By 1294 the Commandery of Ysbyty Ifan (Denbighshire) was united with Halston. By the 16th century Halston had been subsumed into Dinmore in Herefordshire. In 1539 Richard Mytton was granted the lease of the Commandery for five years. The site of the Commandery is that of the Hall of 1690, with later additions. John Mytton, the eccentric drunken foxhunting squire, lived here; he ran through a fortune and died in King's Bench prison in 1835 aged 38. The now privately owned half-timbered Hospitaller chapel is isolated in a field surrounded by yew trees; it dates from 1437-8.

Below and below left: Halston, interior and exterior views of the Hospitaller chapel.

Above and above right: Halston, the Hospitaller chapel.

KINNERLEY

The advowson of the Church of St Mary was appropriated to the Hospitallers before 1248. The Perpendicular west tower survives. The remains of the Norman font are now used as a flowerbed.

Right and below: Kinnerley, the Church of St Mary: the Norman font used as a flowerbed, and the Perpendicular tower.

LYDLEY KEYS

A Templar commandery was founded 1155-60. The land belonged after 1314 to Edmund, Earl of Arundel rather than the Hospitallers. No traces of the buildings survive.

STANTON LONG

The Templars had a camera at Stanton Long. After their dissolution the land (some 100 acres) passed to the Hospitallers at Dinmore. No traces remain.

OTHER

The Knights Hospitaller in 1540 had various other properties in Shropshire including ones at Botley, Chatwell, Clunnbury, Crofton, Enchmarsh (100 acres), Kinlet, Ludlow (60 acres), Preen (100 acres) and Richard's Castle (150 acres).

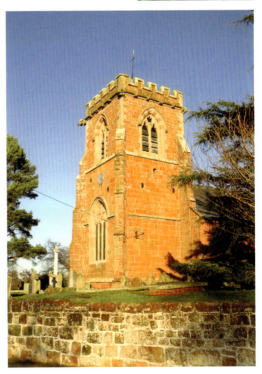

SOMERSET

BRISTOL

The advowson of the Church of Holy Cross belonged originally to the Templars and was part of a commandery at Temple Meads on land granted to them by Robert, Earl of Gloucester. It was transferred to the Hospitallers after 1312. The previous round church was rebuilt as a rectangle in the late 13th century. The bell tower was completed in the 15th century. The church was bombed in the Blitz and now survives as a ruin belonging to English Heritage. A medieval chandelier from the church has been removed to Bristol Cathedral.

BROOMFIELD

The advowson of the Church of St Mary and All Saints was certainly in Hospitaller hands by 1334, and remained with them until the Dissolution. The church is mainly 15th-16th century. It is built of rubble with ashlar dressings. Naves and aisles retain their late medieval roofs. There is a brass of 1443 to the chaplain Richard Silverton who died in 1443. There are

Clockwise from the top: the ruins of Holy Cross, Bristol and its medieval chandelier now in Bristol Cathedral; Broomfield, St Mary and All Saints, interior, exterior and its stained glass.

fragments of medieval glass including an inscription etc to Alice Reskymer, Prioress of Minchin Buckland (1436-57), medieval angels and heraldry.

CHEDZOY

The advowson of the Church of St Mary was appropriated to the priory of Buckland c 1166 but had been lost by the early 13th century. The nave and arcades are of the earlier 13th century, the tower of the 16th. The medieval silvery wooden door with its lozenges is of great beauty.

DURSTON

The advowson of the Church of St John Baptist, in which parish the priory and Commandery of Minchin Buckland were situated, was appropriated to the Hospitallers from 1176. All the church but the tower was rebuilt in 1852-3.

HALSE

The advowson of the Church of St James was given to the Commandery of Minchin Buckland by 1159 and remained with the Hospitallers until 1540. The church has work from the 12th to the 16th centuries including a Norman font.

KILMERSDON

The advowson of the Church of Saints Peter and

Above and right: Chedzoy, the Church of St Mary, interior view and the medieval door.

Below right: Durston, the Church of St John the Baptist.

Below: Halse, the Norman font.

Paul was granted to the Hospitallers for the benefit of Minchin Buckland. The church is 15th century in origin but was heavily restored by the Victorians.

MINCHIN BUCKLAND

In 1166 a small house of Austin Canons was founded here. Because of the murder of a steward this became forfeit to the crown and Henry II in 1186 then granted the lands to the Hospital. A priory was set up, and nuns moved to Buckland from six other houses (Carbrooke, Clanfield, Gosford, Hogshaw, Shingay and Standon). This existed besides a commandery, and the chaplain and steward always came from the Order. The nuns functioned under the rule of St Augustine. In 1227 the Prior of England, Roger de Vere, visited the priory and found discord between it and the Commandery. The nuns seemed to have been fairly grand; in 1232 William, Earl of Arundel, granted 40s a year when his daughter Agnes became a sister. In 1338 there were some 50 nuns who wore a black mantle with a white cross in front. The nuns received a number of donations apart from the Commandery, the earliest being a pension of 13s 4d from Maud, Countess of Clare. In 1500 the Commandery was closed and its lands leased.

In 1535 the priory was valued at some £223 per annum, the richest convent in England. In 1539 the priory was dissolved, and the sisters pensioned off. No traces remain but some of the stone may have been used in the construction of Buckland Farm.

NORTH PETHERTON

The advowson of the Church of St Mary was granted to the Hospitallers by 1186. The church is mainly early 16th century but a 14th century font and a 15th century brass survive. The tower is a tour de force.

Top: Interior and exterior views of the Church of St James, Halse.

Above: Kilmersdon, the Church of St Peter and St Paul.

TEMPLECOMBE

In 1185 Serlo Fitz Odo gave the manor to the Templars. A commandery was set up. The lands were passed to the Hospitallers after 1312. There are apparently scanty remains including that of the chapel at Manor Farm House.

TOLLAND

The advowson of the Church of St John Baptist was given to Buckland Minchin in 1180. The church was built in the 13th century and remodelled in 1871. The font is 12th century.

The Knights Hospitaller in 1540 had various other properties in Somerset.

Clockwise from top left: Buckland Farm, Minchin Buckland; North Petherton, the Church of St Mary, tower, interior and exterior; Tolland, St John the Baptist, exterior, interior and font.

GAZETTEER: SOMERSET

STAFFORDSHIRE

KEELE

An estate in Keele was given in 1168-9 by the Templars. At some stage in the 13th century it became a commandery. After 1312 it was seized by the Crown and remained with Thomas, Earl of Lancaster until his death in 1322. It then reverted to the Crown and was only controlled by the Hospitallers after 1324. They did not establish a commandery there and the manor became part of the Commandery of Halston in Shropshire until the Dissolution. Keele Hall is on the site.

The Knights Hospitaller in 1540 had various other properties in Staffordshire.

SUFFOLK

Above and right: Badley, St Mary's, exterior and interior showing the woodwork.

Below: Battisford, the Church of St Mary and the panels from St John's Manor House

BADLEY

The advowson of the Church of St Mary (near Battisford) seems to have been appropriated to the Hospitallers, and was worth £10 in 1338. The church was made redundant in 1986 and is now in the care of the Churches Conservation Trust. It lies along a rutted track a mile from the road, and is deeply evocative. The tower is c1300. Most of the windows are Perpendicular. The woodwork, both medieval and 18th century, is of great charm. The 13th century font is of Purbeck marble.

BATTISFORD

There was a commandery of the Hospitallers at Battisford with some 200 acres at least as early as the reign of Henry II. The site is that of St John's Manor House; the late 16th century house has a terracotta panel at the base of the chimneystack with the head of St John Baptist on a platter and

another panel dated 1529 with the arms of Giles Russell; the latter was Commander of both Dingley in Northamptonshire and Battisford who was appointed Lieutenant Turcopolier in 1539 but took an annual pension of £100 the next year before dying in 1543. The Hospitallers also had half of the advowson of the Church of St Mary. The chancel and nave are both 13th century.

CAVENHAM

A Templar commandery was dissolved in Cavenham in 1312. No traces remain.

DUNWICH

There was a Templar commandery here by the reign of King John. This was transferred to the Hospitallers after 1312. The church building now lies under the sea with the rest of Dunwich but in 1631 was described by Weever as being a fine building with a vaulted nave and lead covered aisles.

GISLINGHAM

The Templars had a commandery with 100 acres of land from 1150 to 1308. The Hospitallers took over the land. There is no evidence they maintained a commandery. The site is probably that of Manor Farm House.

The Knights Hospitaller in 1540 had various other properties in Suffolk including ones at Coddenham (230 acres), Covehithe, East Bergholt, Great Glemham (50 acres), Manton (100 acres), Mells (70 acres), Preston (225 acres) and Thurlow (120 acres).

SURREY

The Knights Hospitaller in 1540 had various properties in Surrey, but of no great extent.

SUSSEX

POLING

A Hospitaller commandery was founded here before 1199 by Robert Fitz Savarac. In 1338 the Commandery had two knights (Fra' Peter atte Nashe and Fra' Clemens of Dunwich), a chaplain, two clerks and four officials and servants; the land totalled some 317 acres and a dovecote. The Commandery as such seems to have been dissolved in 1445 and the land transferred to support the Grand Prior. The Georgian Fairplace Farm half mile to the north of the centre of Poling has the remnants of the chapel as its east wing. Desmond Seward in his Pimlico *County History Guide to Sussex* writes "Externally, the farm preserves the commandery's outline most convincingly. Indeed, some people claim to have heard the sound of ghostly chanting here while others think they have seen phantom knights who haunt the surrounding fields." A coffin slab survives and is set into the wall at the west end of the house. It bears a Norman French inscription around a large cross: "IHV CRIST: PVR SANTIOHAN: AIT MERCI.

Poling: Fairplace Farm and right, the remnants of its chapel in the east wing.

del alme. berna…" (Jesus Christ, for [the sake of] Saint John, have mercy on the soul of Bern[ard]). The advowson of the Church of St Nicholas, Poling did not belong to the Hospitallers but a similar tomb slab is set into the chancel floor.

SADDLESCOMBE (NEWTIMBER)

In 1228 Geoffrey de Say granted the manor of Saddlescombe with c350 acres to the Templars who set up a commandery there. After 1312 the Earl of Surrey managed to retain the lands for his own use until 1397. Thereafter the Hospitallers maintained a camera there. The site of the Commandery may be where Saddlescombe Manor now lies. The advowson of the Church of St John the Evangelist, Newtimber went with ownership of the Manor. While the church was originally built in the 13th century, Victorian restoration has left nothing medieval surviving.

SHIPLEY

About 1125 Philippe de Harcourt bestowed the manor (some 370 acres) and church of Shipley on the Templars who set up a commandery there. No traces remain. It became Hospitaller after 1312. The advowson of the Church of St Mary was also granted to the Hospitallers. The nave, chancel and tower all date from the middle 12th century although the nave was rebuilt by Pearson in 1893.

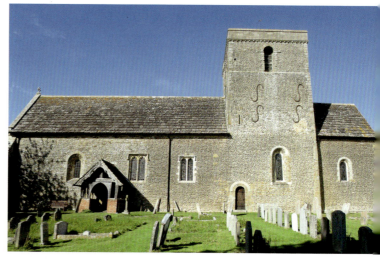

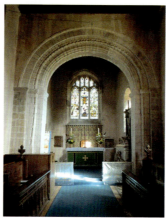

Above: Shipley, the Church of St Mary, exterior and interior views.

SHOREHAM

The Templars acquired land in Shoreham in the 12th century. This passed to the Hospitallers after 1312. In 1325 the land was granted to the Carmelites by the Prior of St John. No traces remain.

SOMPTING

In 1154 William de Braose gave the advowson of the Church of St Mary to the Templars. The nave and chancel of the church were rebuilt shortly thereafter. The transepts were also built in the 12th century. In the 14th century after the church had passed to the Hospitallers a chapel for the Hospitallers was built north of the tower. The Venerable Order of St John has held the advowson of the church since 1963.

SOUTHWICK

Between 1173 and 1189 the advowson of the Church of St Michael and All Angels was given to the Templars, from whom it passed to the Hospitallers. The latter did not appropriate the church but continued to appoint rectors. The chancel contains 13th century lancets, and the nave was rebuilt in the 14th century.

Above: Sompting, the Church of St Mary, exterior, the nave detail of a capital. Above right, the chapel built north of the tower.

Left and below: Southwick, the Church of St Michael and All Angels.

WOODMANCOTE

The advowson of the Church of St Peter was given by Simon le Count to the Templars in the mid 12th century, passing in the early 14th century to Hospitallers. The church is of flint with stone dressings. The north wall of the nave is 12th century. The chancel was reconstructed in the 19th century.

The Knights Hospitaller had various other properties in 1540 in Sussex including ones at Bramber (formerly Templar), Compton (formerly Templar, 140 acres), Eddewarth (formerly Templar, 70 acres), Hickstead (formerly Templar), Icklesham (60 acres), Loxwood (formerly Templar, 100 acres), Midhurst (50 acres) and Ockling (52 acres).

WARWICKSHIRE

RYTON-UPON-DUNSFORD

The Hospitallers held some 300 acres of land here. The Church of St Leonard was appropriated to the Hospitallers. The red nave and chancel date from before 1100. The ashlar west tower is Perpendicular.

SHERBOURNE

The Hospitallers held some 360 acres of land here. The church was appropriated in 1338. The splendid estate church was rebuilt in its totality by George Gilbert Scott in 1862-4.

TEMPLE BALSALL

By 1185 Roger de Mowbray had granted some 640 acres of arable land to the Knights Templar who set up a commandery. Temple Balsall was given land at Chilvers Coton (120 acres), Cubbington, Fletchampstead, Harbury (300 acres), Sherbourne (130 acres), Studley (130 acres), Temple Herdwick (120 acres), Tysoe (500 acres) and Warwick (175 acres). In 1324 the Hospitallers had obtained possession

Woodmancote, the Church of St Peter, exterior and right a detail from the 12th century north wall.

Below: Ryton-upon-Dunsford, Church of St Leonard.

Temple Balsall, the Church of St Mary.

from John de Mowbray and in due course merged it with (Temple) Grafton. Temple Balsall produced two Grand Priors, Roger Mallory in 1443 and John Langstrother in 1470. However the Hospitallers had left Temple Balsall by 1470 as they leased it that year to one John Beaufitz. At the Dissolution it was made over initially to Katharine Parr, the wife of Henry VIII. Elizabeth granted it to Robert Dudley, Earl of Leicester. The Old Hall may contain remains of the Commandery although Pevsner thinks not. It was originally 13th century, built in red brick. The interior contains an aisled hall with timber pillars. The spacious church of St Mary undoubtedly belonged to the Order although it was restored with brutal thoroughness by George Gilbert Scott in 1849. The style is late 13th century and it is built in red sandstone ashlar.

(TEMPLE) GRAFTON

(Temple) Grafton is a misnomer deriving from 1535 as there was never any connection with the Templars. The Hospitallers received a grant of land from Henry de Grafton in 1189. By 1316 they held the manor from Guy de Beauchamp, Earl of Warwick. A commandery was in existence in 1338 but this was later merged with Balsall. No traces of the Commandery itself remain although the dovecote near the privately owned Hillborough Manor two miles to the south was probably Hospitaller in origin. The Church of St Anne belonged to the Hospitallers but is now a building of 1875 by F. Preedy in 14th century style.

WARWICK

A Templar house was founded in Warwick by Roger, Earl of Warwick in the reign of Henry I. It was initially a bailiwick responsible for other Templar lands but after 1185 the Templars made Temple Balsall their main headquarters. The site was across the river from Warwick Castle but no traces remain.

The Knights Hospitaller in 1540 had various other properties in Warwickshire including ones at Barston under Grafton (120 acres), Middleton (60 acres), Morton (60 acres), Newbold (240 acres) and Radford Semele (250 acres).

WILTSHIRE

ANSTY

The land for the Commandery (some 460 acres) was given to the Hospitallers in 1210-1 by Walter de Turberville. (NB the reference in Hardy's *Tess of the D'Urbervilles* to "In the reign of King John one of them was rich enough to give a manor to the Knights Hospitaller".) In the mid 15th century the Commandery at Trebigh in Cornwall was united to it. In 1541 the Commandery went to Sir John Zouche who sold it to the Arundells in the late 16th century. The latter family continued to own it until 1946. The site of the Commandery was at Manor Farmhouse. The fish pond was constructed to provide fish for the Commandery. The hospice was rebuilt at the end of the 16th century and probably resembles its predecessor. The Church of St James dates from c1230 and belonged to the Hospitallers. The transepts were added by the Victorians who also restored the distinctive Hospitaller crosses on the gables. The round font is Norman with its stylised drops hanging down.

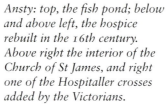

Ansty: top, the fish pond; below and above left, the hospice rebuilt in the 16th century. Above right the interior of the Church of St James, and right one of the Hospitaller crosses added by the Victorians.

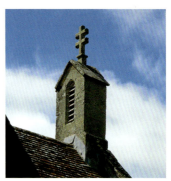

THE KNIGHTS HOSPITALLER IN GREAT BRITAIN IN 1540

Clockwise from the top: Ansty, the Church of St James and its font; Rollestone, the Church of St Andrew, exterior, interior and the font.

ROCKLEY

John Marshal gave some 120 acres in Rockley (Ogbourne St Andrew) to the Templars in 1155-6 who set up a commandery. This passed to the Hospitallers who did not set up a commandery. The land was attached to the Commandery of Sandford-on-Thames in Oxfordshire. No traces remain.

ROLLESTONE

The advowson of the Church of St Andrew rested with the Hospitallers at least from 1302 and remained with them until the Dissolution. The church is small, of flint and stone chequerwork. The chancel and the font are 13th century. There are Perpendicular windows in the nave. The church was fairly heavily restored by the Victorians.

The Knights Hospitaller in 1540 had various other properties in Wiltshire, but of no great extent.

WORCESTERSHIRE

The Knights Hospitaller in 1540 had various properties in Worcestershire including ones at Eldersfield, Feckenham, Hanbury, North Piddle (120 acres) and Temple Laughern

YORKSHIRE

BEEFORD

A moiety of the advowson of the Church of St Leonard was granted to the Templar Commandery at Westerdale and was shared with Bridlington Priory. The fabric is medieval of various centuries. There is a medieval statue of St Leonard on the tower, a 14th century effigy of a priest and a 15th century brass of a priest, Thomas Tonge, appointed by the Grand Prior of the Hospitallers in 1446, who died in 1473.

BEVERLEY

A Hospitaller commandery was established at Beverley in 1201 when Sybil de Vallines, second wife of the the 3rd Lord Percy, made various grants of land. These in 1338 amounted to some 1150 acres. In 1540 Beverley was one of the richest commanderies in England. No traces remain, such as there were having been buried in the 19th century by the construction of the Hull-Bridlington railway.

COPGROVE

The Knights Hospitaller had a manor here with some 190 acres of land in 1338. They also had the advowson of the Church of St Michael by 1309 when the Archbishop of York wrote to the Archdeacon of Richmond "Lately... we passed through the township of Copgrove and beholding the buildings belonging to the Rectory of the church... we observed that they were so greatly dilapidated as to appear deserted and ruinous. We learnt furthermore that the church belongs

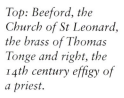

Top: Beeford, the Church of St Leonard, the brass of Thomas Tonge and right, the 14th century effigy of a priest.

to the Hospitallers who are its patrons and have held it for a long time and still hold it. Yet… they show no dread of the penalties attaching to their conduct in this matter. We have taken care to inform you and do now charge you to admonish vigorously…". The church is a simple Norman one.

COPMANTHORPE

William Malbys gave the manor of Copmanthorpe (near York) to the Templars before 1258 on condition a chaplain should be employed to pray for his soul. They set up a commandery. In 1292 the Commandery was responsible for the mills below the castle at York; these had been given to the Templars by Roger de Mowbray prior to 1185. In 1308 it was valued at £80 16s 2d. The manor was transferred to the Hospitallers after 1312. No traces remain.

Above and left: Copgrove, the Church of St Michael.

Below: Darfield, the Church of All Saints.

DARFIELD

A moiety of the advowson of the Church of All Saints was made over to the Hospitallers in 1357. The oldest part of the church is the Norman base of the tower. The nave and chancel are 14th century. The top of the tower is 15th century.

EAST COWTON

Founded in 1142, when Roger de Mowbray granted the Templars various forests, East Cowton (near Northallerton) was probably the first Commandery to be founded in Yorkshire. By 1185 the Templars had some 720 acres of land Edward I stayed there on his way north in 1300. It was valued at c£100 in 1308. It was taken over by the Hospitallers after 1312 but not as a commandery. No traces remain.

FAXFLEET

Little is known of Faxfleet near Hull. It is sited near the confluence of the Ouse and the Trent at the Humber estuary. It was founded on land gifted by Roger de Mowbray in 1185 and was the richest Templar commandery in the county, being worth £290 4s 10d in 1308. Edward I had paid two visits in 1302 and 1303. The lands were not handed over to the Hospitallers; after a period in royal ownership it belonged to the Scropes of Masham. No traces of the Commandery remain.

FELIXKIRK

The advowson of the Church of St Felix was given to the Hospitaller Commandery of Mount St John by one of the Ros family, lords of Helmsley. In 1279 Walter Giffard, Archbishop of

York appropriated to the Hospitallers the rectorial tithes of the parish. The church dates from 1175 although it was much restored by the Victorians. There is a fine Norman chancel arch and a recumbent effigy of a knight.

FOULBRIDGE

Foulbridge was a Templar commandery near Malton, but very little is known about it. It seems to have been founded in the early 13th century. It was worth £254 3s 2d in 1308. It passed eventually to the Hospitallers who did not however establish a commandery there. There are visible remains of the great hall where the Commandery has been incorporated into a farmhouse.

HUNSINGORE

The advowson of the Church of St John Baptist was given to the Hospitallers. The church was totally rebuilt by the Victorians in 1867-8.

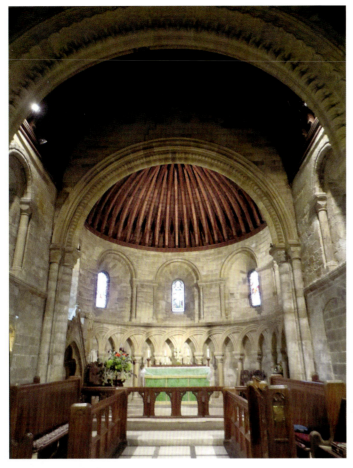

KELLINGTON

The Templars of Temple Hirst were appointing rectors here in 1185. The advowson of the Church of St Edmund was taken over by the Hospitallers and by 1339 they were appointing vicars. The living passed to Trinity College, Cambridge at the Dissolution in 1540. The church was Norman in origin but substantially restored by the Victorians. A "serpent stone" remains from 1340 and a coffin slab of a knight also survives.

KIRKBY FLEETHAM

The advowson of the Church of St Mary was originally given to the Templars but subsequently came to the Hospitallers of Mount St John. The church was completely rebuilt by the Victorians but retains a late 13th century effigy of a knight; this is believed to be of the Templar Sir Nicholas Stapleton, commissioned by his brother Miles after the former's decease. The capitals of the south arcade of the nave are also 14th century.

MOUNT ST JOHN

Early in the reign of Henry I William Percy gave 220 acres of land to the Hospitallers who set up a commandery. By 1338 the buildings were ruinous. A manor house of 1720 (now a dressage centre) has been built on the site.

Opposite page and top: Felixkirk, the Church of St Felix, exterior, the effigy of a knight and the chancel arch.

Above left and right: Foulbridge, the traces of the Commandery incorporated into a farmhouse.

Top: Kellington, the Church of St Edmund.

Above: Kirkby Fleetham, the Church of St Mary, the south arcade of the nave, and left, the effigy believed to be that of Sir Nicholas Stapleton.

NEWLAND

The manor of Newland in Howland was given to the Hospitallers by King John and a commandery was established there in the early years of the 13th century. In 1338 it possessed some 300 acres. The sphere of its bailiwick was extended over time and it became responsible for land in Cumberland, Lancashire, Nottinghamshire and Westmoreland as well as parts of Yorkshire. In 1535 the clear income was £129 14s 11d of which £88 9s 6d was paid to the headquarters of the Order. Various archaeological remains survive on the banks of the River Calder.

NORMANTON

The advowson of the Church of All Saints with 40 acres of woodland was granted to the Hospitallers of Newland in 1256 by Roger le Peytevin. In 1413 Archbishop Henry Bowet transferred the appropriation to Clerkenwell. The church was near the Commandery of Newland. The building is Perpendicular. There are various fragments of medieval and later glass.

PENHILL

This Templar commandery in Wensleydale near the village of Swithinwaite was founded on land given by Roger de Mowbray c 1142.

The land (at least 240 acres) passed to the Hospitallers after 1312. Some ruins of the chapel dedicated to Our Lady and St Catherine together with some stone coffins and an altar survive.

RIBSTON

About 1217 Robert de Ros gave the Templars his manor at Ribston (near Wetherby) and some 900 acres. The Templars acquired further land in the area. A commandery was established. It together with Wetherby were valued at £389.08 in 1308. After the suppression of the Templars this was their only Yorkshire commandery which also remained as a commandery under the Hospitallers. By the 16th century the land was leased. After 1540 the manor went to Charles Brandon, Duke of Suffolk. The (private) chapel of St Andrew is attached to the south east side of the Hall (Carr of York). This appears to have 13th century origins and some fabric of that date. It was dedicated and reconsecrated by the Bishop of Philippi in 1444.

TEMPLE HIRST

The Templar Commandery (the site near Selby, now dominated by the Eggborough power station) originated in the grant of the manor of Hirst in Birkin in 1152 by Ralph Hastings. It possessed some 200 acres of land (16 carucates). In 1308 it was valued at £64 15s 2d. In 1337 it was granted by the Crown to Sir John Darcy. Fragments of the Commandery can be found at Temple Farm including a reset Norman doorway.

Top left and right: Normanton, the Church of All Saints, glass and exterior view.

Above left: Penhill, the ruins of the Chapel of Our Lady and St Catherine, with a stone coffin.

Left: Ribston, a view to the Hall with the chapel on the right.

TEMPLE NEWSAM

The land was granted to the Templars by William de Villiers who died in 1181. The value in 1308 was £174 3s 3d and it was a wealthy commandery with some 16 carucates (2000 acres) of land. The lands did not pass to the Hospitallers but were obtained by the Darcy family. No traces remain. In Bingley a cottage retains a Templar cross.

WESTERDALE

In 1203 King John confirmed to the Templars the gift of Westerdale (near Whitby) with 100 acres from Guy de Bonaincourt. It was valued at £32 19s 6d in 1308. It subsequently became a Hospitaller camera. No traces remain. A medieval packhorse bridge survives just outside the village.

WHITKIRK

The advowson of the Church of St Mary was given to the Templars of Temple Newsam. The church has some 12th century fabric but most dates from the 15th century. It was extensively restored in 1896 and the chancel rebuilt by Bodley at the behest of Lord Halifax in 1901.

The Knights Hospitaller in 1540 had various other properties in Yorkshire including Aislaby,

Alverthorpe (310 acres), Austerfield (270 acres), Kirby (725 acres), Kylwarby (90 acres), Micklefield (72 acres), North Dalton (160 acres), Shafton (40 acres), Shipton Thorpe (40 acres), Skarthingwell (30 acres), Snainton (formerly Templar, 60 acres), Staxton (60 acres), Swanland (20 acres), Swinton (30 acres), Thorn (40 acres), Thorpe Basset (120 acres).

Whitkirk, the Church of St Mary.

SCOTLAND

TORPHICHEN

From the beginning in Scotland the sole commandery of the Hospitallers was at Torphichen to the west of Edinburgh. David I (1124-53) granted in the 1130s "the lands of Torphigan to the Knights of Hospitallers". Further grants of lands and churches followed. Malcolm IV (1153-1164) granted "to God and the Holy Hospital of Jerusalem a toft in every burgh in his kingdom".

In 1128 the Templars had established a commandery at Ballantrodoch, now Temple, Midlothian on the South Esk. Aelred of Rievaulx says David I "committed himself to the counsel of religious men of all kinds, and surrounding himself with very fine brothers of the illustrious knighthood of the Temple of Jerusalem, he made them guardians of his morals by day and night". The ruins of the Temple Church and an archway remain. In about 1187 William the Lion granted them part of the Culter lands (some 8500 acres) on the south bank of the River Dee in Aberdeenshire. A commandery was founded there at some stage between 1221 and 1236; little evidence of their presence remains. In 1287-8 they built a chapel to Mary, the Mother of Christ, known as St Mary's Chapel; fragmentary remnants of this can be found. They were also granted extensive lands in Moray and Nairn. In 1308 the Templars in Scotland were undoubtedly richer than the Hospitallers by approximately half as much again.

Both the Hospitallers and Templars were part of the English priories, which caused problems when Edward I claimed the throne of Scotland. Both the Hospitallers and the Templars supported the English crown during the first stages of the wars of independence. The Hospitaller commander of Torphichen, Sir Alexander de Welles, did homage to Edward I in 1295 and died fighting for him at the Battle of Falkirk in 1298. Their estates were devastated or occupied and the brethren expelled. Robert the Bruce in 1314 was

Top: the remains of the Temple church at Temple, Midlothian.
Above: the remnants of St Mary's Chapel at Maryculter.

however willing to confirm the Hospital in its possessions and privileges, including the lands of the Templars. Sir Ralph Lindsay became the first Scottish Commander. No revenue however reached Clerkenwell until the 1340s. Thereafter the Order in Scotland returned to some kind of solvency.

The position was complicated during the papal schism. The Priory of England via Rhodes remained loyal to Avignon, as did Scotland. However in 1409 the Order transferred its allegiance to the Pisan Pope Alexander V while Scotland remained attached to Benedict XIII. The latter's appointee Sir Alexander de Leighton eventually triumphed in 1418 and was accepted by the Order as Commander. He tried to remove Torphichen from subjection to the Priory of England but this was resisted by the Langue and did not receive conventual approval.

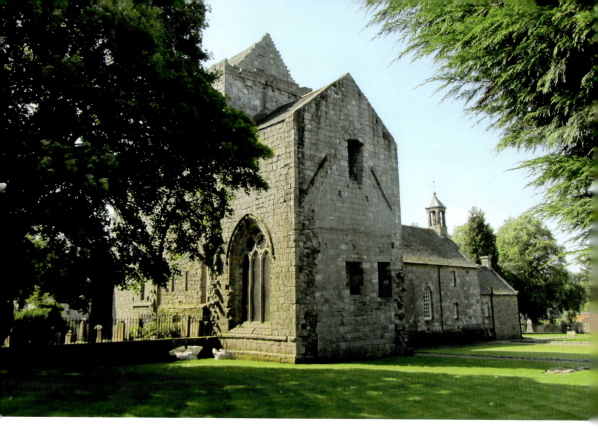

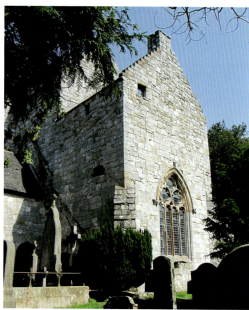

This page and opposite: Torphichen, exterior and interior views of the preceptory church.

Thereafter a modus vivendi was established. Scots alone were appointed to Torphichen but they were not allowed to seek preferment in the Priory of England. Scottish Commanders attended provincial chapters in England.

The Commandery at Torphichen after 1314 possessed property in at least 800 places in Scotland. These were scattered across large areas of the country, but most were in the south, centre and west. The Hospitallers had six baronies (Torphichen, Thankerton (Lanarkshire), Denny (Stirlingshire), Liston (now Kirkliston, Midlothian), Balantrodoch and Maryculter) and a host of smaller properties; the advowsons of the churches of Maryculter, Aboyne, Tullich and Inchinnan were appropriated to them. The estate was described to Queen Mary as "equal to any earl within your Realm". The majority of these properties were leased out. From the mid 15th century the Order's estates were organised into bailiwicks. The baillies were often members of families long associated with the Order – the names of eg Dundas, Lindsay, Meldrum recur. The pre-eminence of the Commanders of Torphichen

is demonstrated by the career of William Knollis, Commander between 1466 and 1510. He sat as a secular baron in Parliament and on the Royal Council, was Treasurer of Scotland during the minority of James IV and saw service on various embassies and royal commissions.

The years 1510-18 (The Battle of Flodden took place in 1513) saw considerable difficulties for the Commander of Torphichen, being part of the English Langue and having allegiance to the Prior of England. However the links between Torphichen and Clerkenwell were restored after 1518. Sir George Dundas was Commander of Torphichen from 1510 to 1532, and Sir Walter Lindsay from 1532 to 1547.

In 1547 Sir James Sandilands was made Commander. He however embraced Protestantism and married Janet Murray. In 1560 the nominal Commandership of Torphichen was bestowed on a cousin. In 1564 Sir James Sandilands surrendered the lands of Torphichen. He received back Torphichen itself and was created Lord Torphichen. He was succeeded by his great nephew, another James Sandilands, from whom the present 15th Lord Torphichen is descended. Sir David Seton may have been the last titular Commander who retired in 1573 with his surviving brethren to Germany, where he died in 1591. It has been asserted that a Scottish poem of the latter half of the 16th century entitled "The Holy Kirk and the Theeves" runs thus:

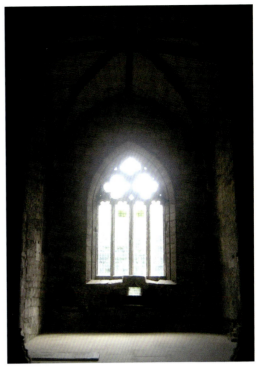

"Fye upon the traitor then,
Quha has broucht us to sic pass
Greedie als the knave Judas;
Fye upon the churle quwhat solde
Holy Erthe for heavie gold;
But the Order felt na losse,
Quhan David Setonne bare the Crosse."

There is no evidence that either Queen Mary or the Scottish Parliament took any steps formally to suppress the Hospitallers.

The nave of the 13th-15th preceptory church at Torphichen was used after the Reformation as the Parish Kirk. The central tower with good carving survives and is now in the care of Historic Scotland.

IRELAND

The Hospitallers received grants in Ireland from the 12th century including that of Kilmainham in 1174 from Richard de Clare, 2nd Earl of Pembroke, known as "Strongbow", where the seat of the Priory was set up. By 1212 the Priory of Ireland possessed at least twelve further commanderies throughout all the Irish provinces except Connaught. This compared with six Templar commanderies.

The Hospitallers were undoubtedly an arm of the Anglo-Norman ascendancy. In the reign of Henry III royal tax collectors were instructed to hand their proceeds to the Prior of Kilmainham for onward transmission to London. In 1274 Prior William FitzRoger was killed in battle against the native Irish. From 1299 onwards four Priors served as Lord Deputy of Ireland. The Hospitallers had far less difficulty in Ireland than in England in getting hold of the lands of the Templars. After 1312 there were at least seventeen functioning commanderies. A number of churches eg Rathmore were appropriated. Kilmainham and Kilteel were effectively castles. Kilmainham was the richest religious house in Ireland.

In the early 14th century the Priors began to be Irish. From 1311 to 1340 the office of Prior was held by the Irish Sir Roger Outlawe, who was also Lord Justice. Thereafter the great Irish families tended to provide the Priors. Sir Thomas Butler, illegitimate son of the Earl of Ormonde, was Prior from 1404 to 1418. In the middle of the century the Priorship was disputed between the Fitzgeralds and the Talbots. In 1494, however, Henry VII imposed the English Thomas Docwra as Prior and ordered that henceforth the Priors should be English. In 1511 Sir John Rawson, the son of a London mercantile family, became Prior.

In the early 16th century the Hospitallers had twenty one commanderies in Ireland as follows: County Dublin (Kilmainham and Clontarf), County Kildare (Kilbegs, Kilhead and Tully), County Carlow (Killergy), County Louth (Kilsaran), County Meath (Kilmainhambeg and Kilmainhamwood), County Down (Ardes), County Waterford (Killbarry, Killara, Crook and Nincrioch), County Cork (Morne or Mora), County Tipperary (Clonmel), County Galway (Kinalkin), County Sligo (Teaque Temple) and County Wexford (Ballyhawk, Kildogan and Wexford).

The Prior Sir John Rawson surrendered Kilmainham in 1540, receiving the Viscountcy of Clontarf and a generous pension of £333 per annum. The priory was briefly revived in 1557 with Oswald Massingberd as Prior.

The site of the Priory of Kilmainham was used by the Duke of Ormond in 1684 to construct the Royal Hospital for military pensioners. The east window of the chapel, dedicated to the memory of King Charles the Martyr, is the sole surviving remnant of the ancient buildings of the Priory.

INDEX OF PLACES

A
Aconbury 76
Addington 37
Althorpe 98
Ambleston 118
Amroth 118
Ansty 136-137
Ashby Parva 95
Ashby-de-la-Launde 98
Aslackby 98-99
Averham 111

B
Badley 130
Baldock 83
Barrow-on-Trent 52
Battisford 130-131
Beeford 138
Beverley 138
Bisham 33
Blakesley 109
Blewbury 33
Bodmiscombe 55
Bosbury 76
Boston 99-100
Bottesford 100-101
Boulstone 76
Brampton Bryan 76-77
Brendon 55
Brimpton 34
Bristol 126
Broadwell 114
Broomfield 126-127

Broxted 59
Buckingham 37-38
Buckminster 95
Bulstrode 38
Burham 86

C
Callow 77
Capel 86-87
Carbrooke 107-108
Cardington 123
Carno 107
Castellan 118
Catmore 34-35
Cavenham 131
Caythorpe 101
Chedzoy 127
Cheriton 64
Chibburn 111
Chilcombe 57
Chippenham 43
Cholesbury 38
Cilmaenllwyd 49
Clanfield 115
Clarbeston 118
Clayhanger 55
Clee St Margaret 123
Clerkenwell 25-26
Copgrove 138-139
Copmanthorpe 139
Cranford 26
Creslow 38-39
Cressing Temple 60

D
Dalby and Heather 96
Darfield 139
Dean 30
Denney 44
Dewsall 77
Dingley 109
Dinmore 77-78
Donnington 101-102
Dover 86-87
Down Ampney 67
Dunwich 131
Durston 127
Duxford 44-45

E
Eagle 102
East Claydon 39
East Cowton 140-141
East Ilsley 35
Eaton Socon 45
Ellesmere 123-124

F
Faxfleet 140
Felixkirk 140
Fordingbridge 73
Foulbridge 140
Friern Barnet 26
Fryer Mayne 57

G
Gainsborough 102

Garway 78-79
Gislingham 131
Godsfield 73-75
Gosford 115
Goulceby 103
Great Limber 103
Great Wilbraham 46
Greenham 35
Guilsborough 109
Guiting Power 68

H
Hackney 27
Haddiscoe 108
Hadlow 87-88
Hallwill 56
Halse 127
Halston 124-125
Hardwick 115
Hareby 103
Harefield 27-28
Harewood 79
Hargrave 109
Hereford 79-80
Hogshaw 39-49
Horkstow 103
Hunsingore 140

I
Ilston 64

K
Keele 130
Kellington 141
Kelmscott 115
Kemeys Commander 107
Kempston (Hardwick) 30
Kidlington 115
Kilmainham 148
Kilmersdon 127
Kinnerley 125
Kirkby Fleetham 141

L
Langford 30-31
Letterston 118
Lincoln 103
Little Maplestead 60-61
Little Staughton 31

Llanfeugan 37
Llanfihangel Nant
  Melan 122
Llanfyrnach 118
Llanmadoc 64
Llanrhidian 65
Llanrhystrad 48
Llansantffraid 48
Llanstephan 49
Llanwddyn 107
Loughor 65
Low Marnham 112
Ludgershall 40
Lydley Keys 125

M
Madron 49
Maltby-le-Marsh 104
Maplebeck 113
Marstow 81
Martletwy 118
Melchbourne 31
Mere 104
Merton 115
Meysey Hampton 69
Minchin Buckland 128
Minwear 119
Mount St John 141

N
Newland 142
Normanton 142
North Baddesley 74-75
North Petherton 128
North Scarle 104

O
Ossington 113
Oving 41
Oxenhall 81

P
Penhill 142-143
Penmachno 43
Penmaen 65
Penrice 65
Poling 131-132
Port Eynon 65-66
Prendergast 119

Q
Quainton 41
Quenington 69-71

R
Radnage 41
Ravensthorpe 110
Rhossili 66
Ribston 143
Riseley 32
Roch 120
Rockley 137
Rodmersham 88
Rollestone 137
Rosemarket 119
Rothley Temple 96-97
Rowston 104
Royston 83
Rudbaxton 120
Ryton-upon-Dunsford 134

S
Saddlescombe 132
Sandford-on-Thames 116
Sawston 47
Sherbourne 134
Shingay 47-48
Shipbourne 89
Shipley 132
Shoreham 132
Sibthorpe 113
Siddington 71
Skirbeck 105
Slebech 120-121
Sompting 132-133
Souldrop 32
South Witham 104
Southrop 71
Southwick 133
Speen 36
St Cleer 50
St Ive 50
Standon 83-84
Stanley 53
Stanton Long 125
Staveley 53
Stebbing 61-62
Stinsford 57
Stretton 123

Strood 89-90
Stydd 94
Sutton St Michael 81
Sutton-at-Hone 90
Swinderby 105
Swinford 97
Swingfield 90-91

T
Temple (Cornwall) 50-51
Temple Balsall 134-135
Temple Bruer 105
Temple Cowley 117
Temple Dinsley 84
Temple Ewell 91
(Temple) Grafton 135
Temple Guiting 71-72
Temple Hirst 143
Temple Newsam 144
Temple Normanton 53
Temple Roydon 61
Temple Southington 75
Temple Thornton 111
Templecombe 129
Templeton 56
The Temple 28
Thorpe-in-the-Fallows 106
Tilmanstone 92
Tolland 129
Toller Fratrum 58
Tonbridge 92
Torphichen 145-147
Trebigh 51
Tregynon 107
Troedyraur 48
Twyford 53

U
Ufton Richard 36
Uzmaston 122

W
Walton East 122
Warwick 135
Welsh Newton 81
Wendy 48
West Peckham 93
West Thurrock 63
Westcott 117

Westerdale 144
Westminster 28
Weston 84-85
Westwell 117
Whitkirk 144
Widmere 42
Willoughton 106
Winkburn 114
Wiston 122
Woodmancote 134
Woolhampton 36
Wormbridge 81-82

Y
Yeaveley 53
Ysbyty Ifan 52
Ystradmeurig 48